Expectant Father Survival Handbook

A Comprehensive Handbook for All Expectant Fathers Out There to Help Your Partner and Yourself during Those Magical 9 Months and Afterwards With Guidelines for Every Step of the Way

By

ANTHONY BLANTON

Respective authors own all copyrights not held by the publisher.

The information herein is offered for informational purposes solely and is universal as so. The presentation of the information is without a contract or any type of guarantee assurance.

The trademarks that are used are without any consent, and the publication of the trademark is without permission or backing by the trademark owner. All trademarks and brands within this book are for clarifying purposes only and are owned by the owners themselves, not affiliated with this document.

Table of Contents

Introduction

Being pregnant is an amazing experience that brings big changes for both partners. The body goes through several symptoms during this period. A person can manage the modifications and know what to accomplish at every stage of pregnancy by being prepared and realizing what to anticipate. However, it is essential to have a medical expert evaluate a pregnancy and adhere to any medical advice to lower the chance of severe symptoms or problems. Consult a doctor about new or strange concerns that develop throughout the pregnancy. Maintaining contact with medical staff may be a crucial source of support in childbirth.

While focusing on your pregnant spouse, don't forget that you also need to care for yourself. Take care of your health by eating well, exercising, managing stress, and getting enough sleep since caring for a pregnant spouse may be exhausting and emotionally stressful. This will make you stronger and better equipped to withstand pregnancy's stress and welcome a new baby into your life.

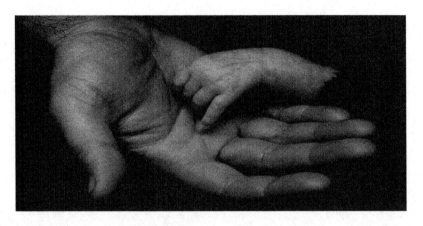

It's common to have prenatal anxiety and worry about the delivery and how it may affect your spouse and the unborn child. Remember that countless individuals carry the baby every day, even though it often seems overwhelming or frightening, and that for many couples, having children is one of life's greatest pleasures.

Speak to your spouse if you need help adjusting to these upcoming changes. Working together and coming up with ideas need effective communication. But most importantly, give yourself space to savor the prospect of being a parent.

When a person becomes a new parent, they are confronted with a variety of challenges that are similar to one another; however, men tend to focus more on financial-related responsibilities, such as wills, college savings, and issues related to the costs of raising a child, which can result in a specific kind of anxiety and stress. According to research, many men experience a roller coaster of emotions when they transition into the position and identity of a father.

It's normal to feel a mixture of pleasure and joy at the prospect of becoming a father, along with some fear about giving up one's independence. Men may feel helpless in light of their recent changes. New fathers may have difficulty juggling their new parental obligations with their desire to advance in their careers. Remember that you are not the only one struggling with uncertainties and worries. It's natural to experience a range of feelings, so you shouldn't beat yourself up if you do. Your partner can help you express your feelings about the major life changes on the horizon by talking to you about them.

It can be challenging for a new father to juggle the many responsibilities of being a parent, a partner, and (potentially) a breadwinner. You suddenly have a lot more work to accomplish, but you only have a small amount of time to complete it. You can learn how to handle it with the help of these tips.

Because newborn infants appear so little and delicate, you might feel more at ease standing back and allowing your partner to take charge of the situation. But you have to take the plunge. The only way to learn and feel comfortable doing things like bathing your baby, changing their diaper, or rocking them to sleep is to do them. If you become involved early on, you will take advantage of an essential opportunity to interact with your child when they are young.

Make the most of every opportunity you have to get back in touch. Take advantage of the fact that your mother can watch your child for an hour by going for a stroll or driving with your partner. If you are the primary provider for your family, you may struggle with guilt when you leave the infant with your

partner to go to work. However, rest assured that you are performing an extremely important duty by providing for your family. Even though you may need the money, there is a better time to seek additional hours or a promotion. Your workload should remain consistent and predictable over the next few months if you delegate duties and concentrate on improving efficiency. You and your spouse will benefit from taking some time to readjust.

Chapter 1: What to Expect When She is Expecting

An unborn child develops for around nine months during pregnancy, also known as gestation. While there may be other signs, missed periods are often the first indication of pregnancy. The average pregnancy lasts for around 280 days or roughly 40 weeks. A newborn's expected date of birth may be estimated with the use of a pregnancy calculator. From conception until birth, we'll go over what to anticipate when your partner is expecting, including typical symptoms, possible problems, testing, and physical examinations.

Although the pregnant woman is in the spotlight for the entire nine months, she must do the most difficult job of dealing with hormone levels and carrying the baby in her womb; that's why her husband's support is crucial during this time. However, coping with their wife's mood swings or particular requirements during these months may be difficult for many expectant dads. A first-time father often feels more anxious than a new mother. They are often overly protective of the mother and the baby since they do not know what is happening before birth. As a result, they might overreact and create chaotic scenarios.

1.1 Recognizing Early Signs

The absence of a menstrual cycle is among the most frequent and reliable early indicators of pregnancy. Pregnancy Association American claims this symptom has been cited by 29% of expecting mothers as the first indication that they were pregnant. In addition to missing menstruation, the following indicators of pregnancy may appear as early as the first weeks after conception:

- nausea, vomiting
- dizziness
- exhaustion
- mild implantation bleeding or spotting
- frequent urination brought on by hormonal adjustments and elevated blood flow via the kidneys
- breast changes like soreness

Some pregnant women have no symptoms, and not every

pregnant woman exhibits the same signs.

Verification of pregnancy

A person may verify that they are pregnant in one of two ways:

- Take a pregnancy test at home.

- See their primary care physician for a checkup and request a blood test for pregnancy.

To determine whether or not a woman is pregnant, a blood or urine sample is analyzed for the presence of the hormone corpus luteum tropin (HCG). HCG may be detected in blood contains many days later a pregnancy has been established.

The hormone levels are low early on in pregnancy and steadily rise during the pregnancy. Multiple pregnancies, as in when expecting twins, maybe triplets, may be identified by having a high amount of the hormone HCG in the blood. An ultrasound of the abdomen or transvaginal region may be performed after a positive pregnancy test.

The scan can verify the following:

- the number of embryos

- the pregnancy's gestational age

- if the positioning before birth is ideal.

1.2 Pregnancy Stages

Doctors use the date of conception to figure out how old the baby is in the womb. They figure out when a person is due by starting to count from the last day of their period to the first day of pregnancy. This covers the time between conception and ovulation. The measurement of pregnancy's gestational age is used in the following instructions. See our in-depth series about how to anticipate each week of pregnancy for additional information.

Weeks 1 to 13

Thirteen initial weeks of pregnancy are considered to be the first trimester. During this time, ovulation and fertilization take place.

Implantation and conception

Conception occurs when the sperm of one man enters the egg of another and fertilizes the female. This often takes place in the fallopian tube of the female after ovulation has taken place. The product of this process is known as a zygote, a single cell composed of both egg and sperm. After this, the zygote begins the cell division process, forming a group of cells known as the embryo.

After completing its cell division and growth process, the embryo will attach itself to the lining, and the uterus will begin to produce venous roots known as villi. The term for this procedure is "implantation." Sometimes an embryo may implant beyond the uterine lining, most often in one of the fallopian tubes. However, this is a rare occurrence that can lead to the development of an ectopic conception. The villi ensure the embryo is securely attached to the uterus's lining when the implantation process goes according to plan. They will ultimately transform into the fetus' placenta and provide nourishment and protection for the developing fetus by adding oxygen and nutrients and removing waste products from the body.

1.3 Early Development

At this stage, the rapid development of the embryo starts to take place. The cardiovascular system, the spinal cord, the brain, and the gastrointestinal tract are the first parts of the body to develop. The placenta starts to take shape at this point. As more time passes, other tissues and organs begin to form. A doctor should be able to sense a pulse by the sixth week of pregnancy.

By week 7, most of the essential organs have already formed. By week eight, the embryo already has, in a much smaller size, everything inside and outside of a grown-up person. The embryo develops into a baby around week 9, continues, and grows around the uterus while encircled via amniotic fluid, which is the water that breaks just before birth. The unborn child reaches its peak size and weight at this stage, around 3 inches in length and 1 ounce in weight (oz).

Possible Symptoms

In the first thirteen weeks of pregnancy, you will most likely have symptoms comparable to the few that may happen in the initial stages, but as the pregnancy progresses, these symptoms may become more severe. At this point of pregnancy, some women may notice weight gain, while others may experience weight loss. Other symptoms that a pregnant woman may experience include mood swings, changes in appetite or cravings for specific foods, headaches, constipation, and heartburn. As a result of the unique nature of each pregnancy, these signs and symptoms do not affect everyone.

Weeks 13 to 28

Lanugo is the fine hair that develops on the head of the fetus during the second month of pregnancy. In addition to that, it starts sucking, and it leaves fingerprints. Eyebrows, eyelashes, sweat glands, and eyeballs begin to take shape at this stage. The brain, other neurological systems, and essential organs are still developing during this stage.

If an embryo is delivered beyond week 22, it could survive with the help of medical intervention. At the end of week 28, the unborn child has around a length of 14 inches and a weight of about 2.15 pounds (lbs.).

Possible Symptoms

Expecting mothers often start to put on weight during the second month of their pregnancy. They may experience the baby's movements, and others may frequently feel them laying their hands on the expecting person's belly in the appropriate places. The second month of pregnancy tends to be a more pleasant time for many pregnant women. In most cases, nausea disappears, and patients report feeling more energized. However, there is still a possibility that some individuals may feel some pain.

Itchiness on the palms of one's hands or soles of the feet, back pain, carpal tunnel syndrome, and swelling in the face, fingers, or feet are all potential symptoms of this ailment.

Suppose the enlargement comes on quickly or is severe. If itching is accompanied by vomiting, jaundice, nausea, lethargy, or lack of appetite, a person should make an appointment with their primary care physician. These symptoms may point to preeclampsia or other issues with the liver. Additionally, some people may notice a change in the color of their skin, as well as the development of stretch marks.

Weeks 29 to 40

The third month begins at week 29 of pregnancy and continues until the week before delivery, typically week 40. The unborn child sees significant growth in size throughout the first several weeks of that phase. Also, the lungs are developed in this phase, and breathing motions will be visible.

Even though they have completed their development, the bones will still be soft. It will start with the eyelids opening. After the 33rd week of pregnancy, it is common for the fetus to move and put its head down to prepare for delivery. It will put on even more weight while shedding its hair in lanugo. After 38 weeks of pregnancy, the fetus has reached its full term. It might weigh anything from 6.75 to 10 pounds and be anywhere from 16 to 19 inches in length.

Possible Symptoms

Throughout this period, you may have the same signs and symptoms as in previous weeks. When a woman is pregnant, she may experience greater back discomfort and have a harder time finding comfortable resting positions. As a result of the pressure that is being placed inside the bladder, they may have to pee more often. Indigestion may also occur if the fetus presses on the stomach while the pregnant woman tries to eat.

Insomnia, hemorrhoids, and breathing difficulty caused by the baby pressing within the diaphragm are other symptoms that may be experienced. Colostrum is an early milk material; thus, the body generates it to be ready for milk supply. Some women may notice that their breasts are leaking colostrum when they get pregnant. It's possible to have early contractions weeks or even days before giving birth. These are what the medical community refers to as contractions that are Braxton-Hicks. No, they don't suggest that labor is imminent.

1.4 Prenatal Care and Check-ups

A woman will go in for routine checkups and examinations throughout her pregnancy to guarantee her unborn child is growing normally.

First Visit

Your first visit will often take place at some time around a pregnancy of eight weeks or beyond. An ultrasound, a pap test,

and the collection of cervical cultures are some of the diagnostic procedures that the physician could use to determine whether or not a woman is pregnant. If there is more than one pregnancy, use ultrasonography to provide that information.

A comprehensive medical history of the patient will also be gathered, and the individual will be examined physically. This involves measuring the individual's blood pressure and testing their urine for evidence of infection or any other abnormalities that may be present. In addition, during the initial appointment, a pregnant woman will have blood examined to confirm her blood type and will be checked for a variety of infectious diseases, including HIV-related liver disease. Another service that a doctor may provide is testing for numerous genetic diseases that may impact the developing embryo.

At this point, the physician will respond to any inquiries the individual could have and provide recommendations regarding safe foods to eat, exercising while pregnant, taking prenatal vitamins, and using safe drugs to take during pregnancy and any additional information the individual should be aware of.

Following Visits

After the first checkup, a pregnant woman should plan to see her obstetrician once per month for the first twenty-eight weeks of her pregnancy. Between weeks 28 and 36, there will be a prenatal visit every other week. Beginning with week 36 and continuing up until delivery, you will have weekly checkups. High-risk pregnancies may need more frequent visits from the expecting mother. During the following appointments, the physician may:

- check an expecting woman's blood pressure

- measure pregnant woman's weight growth;

- take measurements of the belly to see how the fetus is developing

- examine the infant's posture in preparation for delivery at the end of the pregnancy

- do additional ultrasounds (or sonograms)

- conduct additional urine or blood tests

1.5 Routine Tests

Most pregnant women are required to have screening tests during their pregnancy. If a patient has an additional medical condition or is pregnant with a high-risk pregnancy, they may be subjected to additional tests. The following are the most typical types of tests:

- **Screening in First-trimester**

This screening, which takes between eleven and fourteen weeks, looks for cardiac problems and chromosomal abnormalities, including both trisomy 18 and Down syndrome, among other things.

- **20th-week ultrasound**

Around the 20th week of their pregnancies, many women may go for an ultrasound scan to check on the progress of their unborn child. The physician will check for any anomalies and be able to tell the patient the gender of the baby if they specifically ask for such information.

- **Diabetes test**

This screening for pregnancy diabetes takes place between the 26th and 28th weeks of pregnancy. In order to assess a person's blood sugar level, they need to ingest a sugary beverage and then wait for one hour.

- **Urine test**

A pregnant woman would often be asked to provide a urine sample during a checkup screen for potential health complications, such as diabetes, diabetes-related conditions, or preeclampsia.

- **Streptococcus Test Group B**

This screening for a bacterium that may be passed on to

newborns at the time of delivery and may result in a dangerous illness occurs during weeks 36 and 37 of pregnancy and takes place between those two weeks.

1.6 Precautions

Throughout her pregnancy, a pregnant woman will be advised by her doctor to practice caution or refrain from certain activities. This advice will include a wide range of activities.

- **Alcohol**

No quantity of alcohol is considered safe for a woman to drink while pregnant. Consuming drinking causes the unborn child at increased risk for pregnancy, alcohol syndrome, and other birth abnormalities. So, it's best to avoid alcohol altogether.

- **Smoking**

According to a reputable source, this raises the chance of birth deformities and premature labor.

- **Drugs**

Marijuana & other substances increase the likelihood of difficulties occurring during pregnancy and the risk of birth abnormalities in the infant.

- **Fish**

Pregnant people should avoid eating high-mercury fish, such as bigeye tuna or king mackerel, since this might cause birth defects.

- **Overheating**

The likelihood of an abnormal neural tube is increased when a person is overheated. Pregnant women should use caution when the weather is hot or treat fever as promptly as possible.

- **Unpasteurized soft cheeses, uncooked meats, processed meats, greens, and ready salads with poultry salad**

Pregnant women should avoid these foods to limit the chance of catching bacterial illnesses such as salmonella and listeriosis, both of which have the potential to cause damage to the developing baby.

- **Soil**

Infections may be passed on via the soil and through the excrement of certain animals. When gardening or changing the litter in a cat litter box, it is essential to use gloves and wash one's hands before and after the activity.

- **Certain medications**

Several drugs, both those available over the counter and those that need a doctor's prescription, should be avoided during pregnancy. After the 13th week, some may be taken safely. Before taking any drug, a person must consult their primary care physician.

- **Caffeine**

CADO recommends that pregnant women restrict their daily caffeine consumption to less than 200 milligrams (mg).

1.7 Complications

Pregnant women may experience extra things in addition to the standard pregnancy symptoms, some of which may need them to seek medical assistance. This includes things like issues with your teeth and gums, infections of the urinary system, and anemia. Standard medical therapies are available to anyone suffering from these types of diseases. However, depending on the circumstances, a complication may pose a significant threat. Examples include:

- **Infections**

There is a possibility that a woman may have a miscarriage, premature labor, or even a stillbirth if she gets an infection while she is pregnant. This includes getting certain sexually transmitted diseases (STIs). There is a possibility that the child may be born with a birth defect.

- **Preeclampsia**

Whenever this occurs, a pregnant woman's high blood pressure lowers the amount of blood that can reach her baby. If the condition is not treated promptly by medical professionals, the individual may develop eclampsia, resulting in seizures and ultimately leading to a coma.

- **Placenta previa**

This condition arises when the placenta covers all or part of the cervix, the opening through which the baby exits the Uterus.

This problem may resolve itself independently. In such a case, a person will have to have a cesarean section performed instead.

- **Hypertension**

The condition referred to here is elevated blood pressure (hypertension). Because high blood pressure during pregnancy raises the risk of preeclampsia, the individual will need to be watched and may also need medication to bring this under control.

- **Gestational diabetes**

This occurs when a person who did not previously have diabetes acquires diabetes when they are pregnant. It can produce high blood pressure, which may progress to preeclampsia if physicians cannot manage it.

1.8 Tips on How to Reduce Discomfort

Although it is not always feasible to steer clear of the unpleasant signs and symptoms of pregnancy, the following approaches could be helpful:

- **Maintain a healthy weight**

"The phrase "eating for two" does not suggest that a pregnant woman should consume twice as much food as she normally would. Although it is natural for a woman to gain weight during pregnancy, it is recommended by medical professionals that

pregnant women gain no more than 3 to 4 pounds in the second and third trimesters and no more than 2 to 4 pounds in the first trimester. If a woman is pregnant and already has a high body mass index (BMI), she should talk to her doctor about whether or not she should limit the amount of weight she gains throughout her pregnancy.

- **Consume plenty of fluids**

At least two liters of fluids each day, ideally water, is what pregnant women are encouraged to consume by medical professionals.

- **Keep physically active**

Exercising regularly may assist in facilitating labor and delivery and preserving overall health and ideal body weight. Walking and swimming are two hobbies that are often appropriate options. Playing contact sports is generally not recommended by medical professionals.

- **Follow a healthy and balanced diet.**

This entails consuming a diet that is rich in fruits, vegetables, and grains that are whole in sufficient quantities.

- **Take vitamins and supplements.**

Take these in accordance with the directions provided by your doctor. In addition to various other supplements, folic acid, calcium, and vitamin D are often recommended by medical

professionals. If the mother takes excessive amounts of certain vitamins, such as vitamin A, this might pose a health risk to the unborn child. Prenatal vitamins are available for purchase at any drugstore or online at any time.

1.9 Labor and Delivery

Certain signs indicate a pregnant woman is close to giving birth. These could vary depending on the individual. They may consist of the following:

- **Lightening (or dropping)**

The baby settles, or drops lower, into the mother's pelvis at the end of the third trimester. Breathing may have become easier if a baby has fallen in preparation for delivery.

- **Mucus plug**

The body may expel the barrier that shields the uterus from microorganisms. It could seem pink, clear, or bloody. It could have a cork-like appearance. Sometimes people refer to it as a "bloody performance.".

- **Water breaking**

The term "water breaking" refers to the rupture of the amniotic sac, which is a fluid-filled sac that surrounds and protects the developing fetus during pregnancy. The amniotic sac contains amniotic fluid, which provides a cushion for the baby and helps to regulate the baby's body temperature. When the amniotic sac ruptures, the fluid may leak out of the vagina, and this is commonly referred to as water breaking. The amniotic sac rupture can occur spontaneously, often signaling the onset of labor, or a healthcare provider may deliberately rupture it during labor to help speed up the process. It's important to note that not all women experience their water breaking before or during labor, and some may have a slower leak of amniotic fluid instead of a sudden gush. If a woman's water breaks, she should contact her healthcare provider immediately to determine the best course of action for the mother and baby's health.

- **Effacement**

Effacement is a term used to describe the thinning and shortening of the cervix during pregnancy in preparation for childbirth. The cervix is the lower part of the uterus that connects to the birth canal and normally measures around 2-3 centimeters in length. As the baby grows and approaches full term, the cervix undergoes changes that allow it to open and the baby to pass through. One of these changes is effacement, which is often expressed as a percentage. For example, if the cervix is fully effaced, it means that it has thinned to the point where it's no longer detectable and has stretched out to become part of the uterine wall.

Effacement is typically measured during a vaginal exam and is important in determining when a woman is ready to deliver. It's important to note that effacement can occur before dilation and that the rate at which effacement and dilation occur can vary widely between individuals. Healthcare providers monitor effacement during labor to ensure a safe delivery and may recommend interventions if effacement is not progressing as expected.

Dilation

Dilation in pregnancy refers to the opening of the cervix, which is the narrow passage that connects the uterus to the birth canal. During pregnancy, the cervix is tightly closed and long to support and protect the developing fetus. However, as the baby grows and approaches term, the cervix gradually softens and shortens, and the uterus muscles begin to contract. This process, known as labor, causes the cervix to dilate, or widen, allowing the baby to pass through the birth canal and be born. Dilation is measured in centimeters, with 10 centimeters being fully dilated and the ideal size for the baby's head to pass through. It's important to note that every woman's labor and delivery experience is unique, and the rate of cervical dilation can vary greatly. Healthcare providers monitor cervical dilation during labor to ensure that both the mother and baby are progressing safely and to make informed decisions about interventions if necessary.

Contractions

The many forms of closures are as follows. Practice pains are what Braxton-Hicks contracts are. They are erratic and don't signify work. However, labor may be indicated if the cramps are frequent, consistent, move closer between, and then last more.

1.10 Stages of Labor

Every woman's labor experience is unique. In general, there are several stages of labor during vaginal delivery:

- **Early labor**

The cervical causes vasodilation to 3-6 cm during this stage, which lasts roughly 8–12 hours. The convulsions often don't hurt much. They could last between five and thirty minutes and around thirty to forty seconds.

- **Active labor**

The pelvis dilates beyond 7 cm during this stage, which lasts around 3–5 hours. Those who have an epidural could spend more time in this stage. Contractions typically last 45 to 60 seconds, followed by a three-to-five-minute break.

- **Transition**

Again, until the membrane dilates to 8 mm, this stage occurs for around 30 to 30 minutes. There will be more prolonged and powerful contractions. They could last for 60 to 90 seconds with 30- to 2-minute pauses.

- **Pushing**

The pushing period often lasts between 20 and 2 hours. Constant contractions that last 5–90 milliseconds alternate with 3-minute pauses. A person will have a strong desire to press throughout the contractions. Crowning is the term for when the baby's head starts to emerge. One could get a burning feeling. The doctor will instruct the patient to cease trying, and the baby will be delivered.

1.11 What You need To Do?

Helping the expectant father in this journey is just as important as the expectant mother. Here are some tips for surviving your wife's pregnancy:

Be informed

To understand what your spouse will experience each month,

read up on baby in books and online. A future father must learn about pregnancy so they can react appropriately if their future wife has nausea or dizziness. If the partner has learned about the circumstances of pregnancy, she will recognize that it is common and frequently occurs in pregnant women; you should help her feel better by supplying water and helping her relax. Usually, people try home remedies and ayurvedic medicines to soothe the woman.

Hear her out

It can be daunting to be pregnant and give birth, particularly if it's your first kid. Tell your partner that she is welcome to vent with you about anything, even her worries about an impending sonogram or whether or not she will be a good mum. Making her feel a bit better and assuaging her anxieties. However, it's equally crucial for you to express your thoughts and worries. After all, you two work as a team, and supporting each other is important during this critical time.

Accompany her to the doctor's

Place doctor's appointments in your diary. In any case, traveling with her to the maternity doctor's visit will not only provide her with moral support but will also make it easier for her to comprehend the changes that are happening in her body. Additionally, it will allow you to seek professional guidance on all your pregnancy-related questions.

Plan a babymoon

The third trimester is your greatest chance to enjoy the maternity glow, but the first trimester may make your spouse anxious due to motion sickness and nausea. This is a popular time to go on a "babymoon" or this last pre-baby trip.

Do couple activities

Join your partner on her nighttime strolls, then work out together. Prenatal yoga classes are also available for expecting couples. "Even I would carry out the exercises my wife was instructed to perform while carrying our first child. The key is spending a lot of time together since you can see the baby's motions.

Offer help

Your partner would be emotionally fragile and physically exhausted throughout these months. So instead of her calling out to you, be extra kind and offer to help. Please make a list of things you need to do for yourself, such as cleansing the home more often or going to the store right away, and help ensure to cross them off as you manage your timetable.

Indulge her

Recognize that your wife is expecting a child and is not ill. Consider strategies to make her feel better. You may prepare her favorite meal or snack or go out to supper with candlelight. It's a good idea to spice up your friendship now since after the kid is born, you can be sure that the first few days will mainly include spending late nights caring for the infant's demands.

Get ready

Ensure your wife's birthing bag is prepared as the last few stages of the pregnancy get nearby. Make a list of the family members whose contacts you must provide when the baby is born. Additionally, baby-proof your home and have all the necessities on hand before the mother and the child return from the hospital, such as clothing, diaper bags, and medications.

1.12 Why Supportive Partners Are Important

Today, more than ever, a pregnant woman's partner is encouraged to be actively engaged. No more cigars in the exam room while your spouse is occupied with giving birth to your new kid. Of course, someone else may carry your kid to term and give birth, but there are still many ways for you to participate. Your participation may benefit your connection with your spouse, your general well-being and health, and that of your unborn child.

According to published research, pregnant women who did not yet have their partners' support also had greater levels of depression and sadness and were more likely to smoke. This prompted the researchers to conclude that having a supportive spouse may be crucial for both the wellness of pregnant women and the development of their fetuses.

A crucial and possibly changeable focus for treatments to enhance pregnancy outcomes might be partner support. Another published research investigated the effects of partners' financial and emotional assistance on mothers' "felt stress" during birth. Mothers' stress levels were "strongly associated" with having a financially and emotionally committed husband. Additionally, there is a high correlation between partners attending prenatal checkups and mothers' reduced stress levels. The researchers note that pregnant women's mental health affects the unborn child's health. Pregnant women's perceptions of stress might result in negative reproductive outcomes that could endanger the mother's and unborn child's physical and mental well-being.

How Can Partners Provide Support?

There is no doubt that many people want to help their pregnant partners but are not sure about how to do it. They could need clarification about how best to intervene and what their spouse wants or needs. It never pays to inquire, to start with. One of the first actions you can do when you consider helping your mate is to establish open communication channels about their requirements through every pregnancy phase.

1.13 Partner Support Tips

Educate Yourself

The more you understand your partner' changing bodies, how this may effect their physical and psychological moods, and what types of challenges they may be facing, the better you'll be able to support and assist them. The same is true for your baby's healthy growth and development and how to prepare for and after labor. These topics should be on your radar as well as your partner's.

Talk and Share

When something relates to business assistance, open communication is necessary. You want your spouse to feel comfortable talking to you about everything, including difficult things.

Get Involved

Simply showing up can be one of the most important ways to assist someone. Attend all of your partner's medical visits. Participate in choices on the prenatal diagnosis you may wish to have, the health insurer that is best for your family, and the location of your delivery. Go to whatever childbirth or parenting courses you decide to enroll in, too.

Ask The Right Questions

You are only expected to sometimes be aware of what your spouse needs. Asking what can be done for your spouse is nothing to be frightened of. There are going to be many ways you can help, from making sure they have scheduled medical visits to deliver them back massages to preparing their favorite nutritious food.

On the other hand, you want to avoid putting the onus on your mate and expect that to be the person who directs your every move. Taking proactive actions to help their spouse is crucial to being a have certain. It's crucial to educate oneself about pregnancy and the challenges your spouse may be experiencing.

Chapter 2: Supporting Your Partner Through Emotional and Physical Challenges

Making decisions with the pregnant person's consent and in the family's best interests necessitates an active support team. Your spouse may feel safer if you participate actively in the labor and delivery process, and it may also make you feel valuable and involved. Additionally, active assistance may speed up labor, lessen the need for painkillers, and reduce invasive surgery. Additionally, it may result in increased bonding and birth process pleasure.

Labor and delivery may be improved by having a supportive companion. Individuals are less inclined to see their delivery as traumatic when they feel supported. Nevertheless, a man can go through a traumatic delivery as well, and having a partner by their side may help them deal with it and make them feel less alone in the process. A positive birthing experience prepares a couple to collaborate to overcome the problems of parenthood.

On the other hand, inadequate assistance may make a person giving birth feel vulnerable and alone. According to her, it could even be a factor in why they find the delivery traumatic. The expectant mother may feel cut off if the partner is not encouraging. When women feel helpless, their bodies automatically go into the fight-or-flight position. This may physically slow down labor's development, which may influence the number of required interventions and the mother's and baby's overall safety during delivery.

2.1 Emotional Changes and Preparations

You and your partner are going to have a child. Although expecting a baby could be among the most difficult periods in life, it also ranks among the most wonderful and joyous moments. Along with a whirlwind of emotions, your pregnant spouse will undergo a severe storm of changes as their body adapts to the developing baby.

You may well be worried about what your involvement in all of this will be, what the most important pregnancy facts are, and if you'll be able to be the kind of great wife you want to be. Following that, it's all about gaining as much knowledge as you possibly can about labor and childbirth, taking part in as many as you can, listening well, and, of course, being ready to rush out and grab your spouse whatever strange cravings they're wanting, no matter what time of the day. Is anyone for pickles and ice cream?

2.2 How to Prepare

Even before labor really starts, you can help your spouse. You may want to assist them in making their homebirth more comfortable or talk to them concerning their desires for anything from painkillers and medical procedures to who she want in the birthing room and how she feels about nursing. Start by discussing the distribution process in a childbirth education class.

Emotional Support

It's important to be adaptable and to avoid taking your partner's actions or words personally if you want to be a good supportive partner during labor. Throughout the process, your role could vary. Be willing to take on various jobs and provide assistance in many ways.

Because labor is arduous, you can take on some of your partner's discomfort, stress, and irritation. Accepting this may be difficult, but keep in mind that they are going through a very tough period and may say or do things out of pain. Instead of taking things personally, work on letting them go.

Physical Support

Additionally, you may be ready for delivery by learning about the stages of labor, being aware of your choices and what to anticipate, and getting a clear understanding of the preferences of the person giving birth so you can assist them as best you can. Additionally, you may learn how and when to push hard for pain relief, hold children, and support them physically. Additionally, experts advise educating oneself on the connection between oxytocin and labor. Understanding the phases of labor and being aware that the person giving birth needs to relax, remain hydrated, and eat are also useful.

Preparing for Challenges

It's also important to understand that offering assistance to others might be difficult. It is difficult to see somebody you care about suffering. Your natural impulse may be to attempt to "fix" it. It's crucial to keep in mind that labor discomfort is natural and nothing to be afraid of. Keep in mind that labor is a normal procedure. Help the expectant parent keep this in mind and maintain their calm; this will cause the labor to go faster and with less pain. It's also crucial to remember that it's typical for labor to last a long time. Long hours are sometimes good hours.

Additionally, labor will evolve and strengthen during the procedure. The laboring methods that were helpful in the early stages of labor may be less useful in the active or transitional stages. Try out several methods, including counterpressure, massage, hip compresses, effleurage, maintaining calm surroundings, and assisting the delivering parent in shifting positions.

2.3 How To Comfort and Support Your Partner

Childbirth instructors occasionally use the abbreviation SUPPORT to refer to helping your partner during labor. According to them, this stands for a comforting atmosphere, urinating, changing positions, praise, oxygenation, relaxation, and touch. Here are a few more suggestions for helping your spouse during childbirth.

Encourage Them to Use the Bathroom

According to experts, you must encourage your partner to urinate once per hour. This facilitates maintaining a dry bladder, allowing the baby more space to enter the cervix and hastening the course of labor.

Create a Supportive Environment

Check to see if the room is pleasant, well-lit, and comfortable. Additionally, try your best to keep the area clean and free of waste and clutter. Make sure your partner is alright with you playing light music. You might also work to limit guests to ease the tension in the environment. Provide hydration in the manner of popsicles, ice chips, water, or clear drink. Because their bodies keep working so hard, expecting women should drink lots of water. Simple acts of support, such as helping your wife stay hydrated or preparing a fresh smoothie, are very appreciated.

Help Them Change Positions

Changing the positions during labor may aid in altering the pelvic shape, which is crucial for the baby's ability to pass through the birth canal. Additionally, it gives the pregnant woman a new "feeling" and helps lessen labor pain. Every 30 to 60 minutes or so, gently recommend the person giving birth change positions and assist them in doing so. It can include persuading them to lie on their side or having them do a supported squat while exerting counterpressure on their lower back.

Encourage Breathing Exercises

It's crucial to maintain good oxygenation throughout labor and delivery. Breathing allows both the mother and the baby to remain properly oxygenated and helps them concentrate on getting through one spasm at a time. You must assist your spouse in breathing through their contractions for this reason.

Use Touch

Back labor sufferers may find comfort by using compressed nitrogen during a contraction. Touch stimulates the brain, which may shut the "gate" and reduce the number of pain impulses that reach the brain. Additionally, it aids the mother in finding their "posture of ease." The mother may support cervical dilatation and labor progression with their contractions more successfully if they are not holding stress in their bodies. Experts recommend that the support worker use Crave Baby Moisture Cream to gently massage the laboring woman in the early stages of labor to induce calm. The body needs the energy to maintain the endurance of birth. As a result, resting whenever possible is quite beneficial for the mother.

As I pointed out previously, childbirth and labor may be traumatic events. You could feel scared and think about all the things you can do to help your spouse, which is natural. But with some planning, your partner will greatly appreciate your help and support. Additionally, offering assistance has several advantages, including a reduction in the number of medical interventions and a reduction in labor duration.

Offer Praise and Encouragement

Tell your spouse how pleased you are with them and what a terrific job they are doing. Remember to compliment them often during labor, as this reassurance will become more crucial when labor gets more difficult. They need to be aware of your support and your faith in them.

Support during labor and communication increases labor comfort. Interestingly, Gate Management Science of Pain claims that whenever we give a person experiencing pain something else to think about—for example, touch, smell, sound, or taste—those sensory experiences travel faster toward the brain than just the sympathetic nerves, closing the "gate" and not allowing as many distress signals through.

In addition, one of the most helpful things a partner can do is provide verbal support. Verbal encouragement may shorten labor on its own without the need for any additional methods.

Promote Relaxation

To assist your spouse in adopting a relaxed posture, it's crucial to encourage relaxation techniques. The baby may be pulled in and down more forcefully during contractions if the laboring parent can maintain a relaxed position, which puts pressure upon that cervix and speeds up labor.

Remember that your purpose in being there is to support and act as an advocate for the person you assist throughout labor and delivery. Additionally, it is crucial to be organized. This could include asking questions or providing your partner with whatever they need to feel supported. Also, you want to confirm that you are alert and prepared for the experience. Helping your spouse during labor can be greatly helpful if you can react to requirements right away.

2.4 Sex During Pregnancy

During pregnancy, it's typical to discuss sex with your spouse. You should be aware that having sex when your spouse is pregnant is safe unless your partner's doctor advises otherwise. However, since the situation changes constantly, several things must be considered:

- As your partner's body changes, certain positions could be difficult for them. Go slowly and be patient as you explore to find the positions that feel good for both of you.

- Communication is key. Try to communicate with your spouse if you're not sure about what they want or don't want sexually. Now is a fantastic time to have an open conversation about sex and learn more about your partner's sexual preferences.

- Sometimes your spouse could beg for more sex, but other times they may not be interested. Don't take this personally; your partner's interests often change during pregnancy.

- If you're worried about your partner's lack of desire for sex, remember that this is fairly frequent for pregnant women as their pregnancies develop and often go away after the baby is born (or at least a few months old!). Pregnancy and postpartum are a season in life, like everything else, and they pass and change like everything else.

2.5 Trimester by Trimester Breakdown of Partner Support

Even the fact that everything seems to change rapidly during pregnancy may make it a bit of a crazy ride. Your partner will only be allowed to drink white bread and soda water for one month. They'll want to eat whatever they see during the next month. He following is what to anticipate from one phase to the next and up to her baby's delivery.

First Trimester

Physical Support

For your spouse, the first trimester may be quite physically taxing. Even if they don't "appear" pregnant, their bodies undergo substantial hormonal and physical changes. They could feel worn out, queasy, lightheaded, or even throw up (perhaps a lot!). They'll also have a distinctive palate. They may crave things they've never tried before, while other meals will make them throw up.

Here, your objective is to spoil her as much as possible. Allow them to sleep in, take naps on the weekends, and never consume anything near them which might make them sick.

Your duty may also include bringing them a yuck bucket. Although these weeks might be incredibly demanding, they will be gone before you even realize it.

Emotional Support

You might also anticipate moodiness and a few gloomy and worrisome sensations while your spouse is trying to adjust to the changes in their bodies, their identification, and the surge of hormones that occur during the first trimester. Typically, your partner wants a good, understanding ear and extra love and affection.

Second Trimester

Physical Support

The second quarter of pregnancy is typically called the "honeymoon" stage. Typically, your partner's expanding body has not yet grown too uncomfortable, and the horrendous symptoms from the first fortnight have subsided (although some women, regrettably, have nausea for much of their pregnancies). Moms often have their largest appetites during this trimester.

Your partner's needs may now be your top priority. Late-night supermarket runs for specific cravings may become a habit. The second trimester is a fantastic time to encourage your spouse to have a healthy diet and lifestyle. Combining your efforts may be beneficial. Along with your spouse, you may acquire healthy habits; begin preparing better food with them, go on hikes together, refrain from tobacco and alcohol, etc.

Emotional Support

Typically, your spouse feels joyful and anticipatory at this phase as they come closer to receiving their child. She could be feeling overburdened by her growing list of tasks, her potential future baby event, and the significant 20-week ultrasound scan that is rapidly approaching. She may benefit greatly by participating in the preparation and future activities. Remember that you are also affected by her motherhood and the child.

Third Trimester

Physical Support

Your spouse can feel extremely uncomfortable again during the third trimester. Her expanding baby's weight might be quite taxing. They could have backaches, sciatica, discomfort in the round ligaments, and sometimes even Braxton Hicks contractions which don't really cause labor. If you don't know what they are, Braxton Hicks contractions are "false" labor pains experienced by a pregnant woman before the "real" labor. Additionally, they could feel heartburn and swollen feet.

Emotional Support

It's time to start getting ready for your baby's impending arrival, which may be both thrilling and highly stressful. As labor and delivery approach, you will both have many questions. Prenatal checkups will happen more often, so if you haven't already, now is the time to prioritize them.

Being a good listener at this time is important since your spouse likely has normal concerns about giving birth and recovering after giving birth. In addition, ensuring they have everything they need and preparing for the baby can relax them psychologically and make them much less concerned. Once again, being present, paying attention, and rushing about town to get any last-minute supplies are all wonderful things to do now.

2.6 How Partners Can Bond with Baby During Pregnancy

There are many ways a non-pregnant spouse may develop a close relationship with their unborn child, from attending prenatal courses to listening to music together in utero. Here's how to get to know your child even before they are born.

Although many studies have shown that bonding with your baby when they are still in the womb may be a deep and helpful experience both for the parents and the baby, few parents realize the value of doing so. The issue is that unless the baby is developing inside from her stomach, it may be harder to feel connected to them.

Prenatal bonding is still possible even if you never feel morning sickness or fetal activity. It will take a little work—and imagination—on your side. To get you started, we've asked professionals and parents with experience to give their suggestions for establishing a connection with the unborn child.

Think Ahead to the Adventures You'll Share

A pregnant woman frequently visualizes an infant when she thinks about her unborn child. Greg Bishop, the creator of Training Camps for New Dads, argues that parents, in contrast, can imagine the child as an older child and a new playmate eager to be introduced to the outside world. According to Greg Bishop, "creating or purchasing something related to all of those things is a tangible approach to cement this budding link" because parents frequently daydream about activities they will do with their children when they get older. "Perhaps it's a miniature fishing pole, or maybe it is related to their favorite sports team," one may imagine.

Attend Your Partner's Prenatal Appointments

Attending maternal hospital appointments can be one of the best ways to remain connected with your partner's pregnancy. You can get updates on the baby's growth, ask questions, and help your spouse through any pregnancy-related difficulties. Additionally, you'll be among the first to your baby's heart and witness ultrasounds in real-time, both of which are unforgettable memories. Get a copy of the photo of the baby to show to your loved ones and close friends. When you first see this undeniable proof that a baby is actually on the way, it's normal to feel emotional.

Get to Know Your Baby Gear

Once you've taken your baby home, you'll have to get used to a lot of new equipment. Refrain from letting your spouse figure everything out on their own. Instead, familiarize yourself with the fundamentals to reduce the uncertainties of those early days. According to experts, researching baby items, like a breast pump, may benefit your spouse and your newborn child. It also gives you a sense of empowerment.

According to experts, knowing what to anticipate can open up many promising options before the baby even comes. You won't regret being an expert in using your baby's equipment before those fuzzy newborn days set in, from fitting the car seat to arranging the packed 'n' play and using the bottle warmer.

Sing a Duet

For those in the good family: Why not perform duets for the unborn child with your partner? Everyone engaged will receive the uplifting musical energy permeating the amniotic environment. At 16 weeks gestation, according to experts, babies hear noises from the outside world. They can also distinguish their parents' sounds even before birth. Baby will recognize the melody, become calm, and turn to dad if daddy sings to it when the child is still inside the womb." Before going to sleep, begin a singing pattern; you may carry on the custom even after having a child.

Play DJ to Your Partner's Bump

Make your future kid the perfect playlist, and then play it in their snug cave. Specifically, carefully wrap some headphones over your partner's growing tummy. This is your opportunity to instill in your child a love of excellent music and turn them into lifelong listeners. But Katherine Cox, a preschool music instructor, cautions against turning it too loud: "The hearing of fetuses and newborns is incredibly sensitive, so the sound volumes we expose kids will need to be on the soft side." Consider the music you're playing for the baby as well. While harsh, clashing tones might stress a newborn, classical music, soft lullabies, and a soothing melody can relax a baby. So, wait till they're a little older to introduce them to your favorite hard rock or metal songs.

Encourage an Early Love of Literature

It's never too early to influence your unborn child's literary preferences by reading them in utero since they have ears. They'll do better the sooner you get out the books.

Take the Baby on a Virtual Road Trip

While some of your kin will undoubtedly live far away, you may still send some in-utero pleasantries. Introduce your infant to the voice of your sister or your grandma in California or Oklahoma. It will feel even more genuine if you let the outer world know how excited you are to become a parent. Your child may be better prepared within the next few months when they are old enough to go on their first major car trip.

Feel for Baby Movements

According to the life coach, "My wife and I would stay around every evening of the last several months when our kid was the typical bun-in-the-oven and monitor his motions as if we were passionately enthralled students of basketball at the Cup Finals. A Fellow of both the Academy of Qualified Maternity Educators and a Lamaze Trained Childbirth Educator may approve of this since she says: "Having dad lay his hands on mom's developing tummy is a simple way for him to feel the sensations of the baby.

It's entertaining to attempt to guess which part of the baby you are feeling—their foot, knee, finger, head, or bottom. Dads find it surprising that their infants may even "play" with them by punching or where their hands are placed."

2.7 Your Complete Dad-to-Be Cheat Sheet and Guide

Congratulations on becoming a father! With these instructions, advice, and ideas, you can handle parenthood for the first time. Being a father is not difficult, but it is not the most straightforward task in the world. By reading commonly asked questions, you may get a head start on the game, and then when your child is born, you can demonstrate your improved fathering skills. Never before has being a parent been so simple!

How Can I Get Ready for Childbirth and Labor?

Even if your spouse is giving birth, it's common for expectant fathers to have anxiety. Study up on the phases of labor, take advantage of a free view Showing the region where deliveries are made, attend a class given by the facility or your care facility, and learn about pain-relieving techniques for the pregnant woman. The more at ease you are when it occurs, the more acquainted you will be considering your environment and what to anticipate for each point in labor.

How Do I Prepare a Bottle?

Learn how to make a bottle before leaving the hospital if you are completely independent of nursing. Heat it to nearly 98.5 degrees Fahrenheit; check the temperature with a digital thermometer or your bottle warmer's temperature monitor. You might reheat the bottle using a device or another technique. Follow the process to avoid questioning your wife/partner,

"Honey, how does the thing work?" at 4 a.m.

What amount should my child eat?

The amount needed for feeding is relatively little, and it changes throughout the first day to bring life, according to Sunny Dickinson, a Yoga Certified Birth Education plus a DONA

Internationally certified doula for birth. "It is imperative to remember that somehow a baby's mouth is quite tiny," she adds. For instance, experts say a newborn's stomachs are around the size of a cobblestone and can retain approximately one teaspoon a day after birth. By day ten, a baby's stomach is roughly the size of a huge egg and can accommodate around four tablespoons of food, the author continues. Babies should seem satisfied after a feeding. If a baby is unhappy after a meal, experts advise burping and giving the mammary and bottle again.

How many soiled diapers should I anticipate?

A newborn should be wearing at least one diaper change. Once at the start of the day, it can lead to 5 to 6 diapers daily. However, the number of dirty diapers will differ somewhat depending on whether the infant of breastfed or given formula. In the first week, it's generally recommended to have one dirty diaper every day the baby has been alive (one dirty feces day one, one from day one, etc.) until after five or six days. A breastfed infant has one to twelve tiny stools after this.

There will also be variations in how Baby's stool looks. As the mother's milk transforms from serum mature milk, the color of a breastfed baby's poop will vary, ranging from dark green to beige mustard yellow. A formula-feeder infant may have less, bigger, more formed, tan-colored poop.

The Scoop on Poop: What's Normal, What's Not

Once your kid has had enough changing, you will have a filthy diaper to deal with. Some individuals have a system for disposing of used diapers, while others use cloth diapers that need washing. Before things get out of hand, plan what you're about to do and be prepared.

Diaper Changing Procedure?

One of the most important responsibilities of being a dad can include changing the diaper. Diaper changing can be daunting for new dads, but with a little practice, it can become a simple routine that you and your baby will get used to. For it's an important matter, we will discuss the diaper changing procedure step by step to help you get started.

Step 1: Preparation

Before changing your baby's diaper, you need to have all the necessary supplies within reach. Have everything ready and easily accessible so you don't have to leave your baby unattended. You will need a clean diaper, wipes, diaper rash cream (if needed), and a changing pad or clean towel.

Step 2: Place your baby on the changing surface

Place your baby on the changing surface (changing table, bed, or floor) and secure them with a strap or arm. Make sure that the surface is clean and flat. Never leave your baby unattended on the changing surface, even for a second.

Step 3: Remove the soiled diaper

Open the tabs of the soiled diaper and lift your baby's legs by their ankles, keeping their bottom elevated with one hand. Use the other hand to wipe the area gently with a wipe, removing any poop or pee. You may need to use several wipes if it's a messy diaper. Be sure to wipe in the direction from front to back for girls to prevent any bacteria from spreading. For boys, cover their penis with a wipe to avoid getting peed on.

Step 4: Clean the diaper area

Use a clean wipe to clean the diaper area thoroughly. Pay

attention to skin folds and creases to avoid any rashes. You can also use a washcloth, or cotton balls dipped in warm water to clean the area, especially for newborns. Once you have cleaned the area, let it air dry for a few moments or use a clean cloth to pat it.

Step 5: Apply diaper rash cream (if necessary)

If your baby has a diaper rash, you may want to apply some diaper rash cream before putting on the new diaper. Apply a small amount to the affected area, being careful not to overdo it. The cream will help soothe and protect your baby's skin.

Step 6: Put on the new diaper

Slide a clean diaper underneath your baby, ensuring the tabs are at the back. Bring the front of the diaper up between your baby's legs and secure the tabs on the sides. The diaper should be snug but not too tight. You should be able to fit two fingers between the diaper and your baby's tummy.

Step 7: Clean up and wash your hands

Dispose of the dirty diaper and wipes in a diaper pail or trash can. Wash your hands thoroughly with soap and water to prevent the spread of any bacteria.

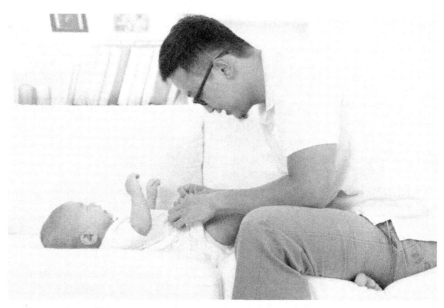

What Should Be in Diaper Bag??

Basic diaper bag items include diapers, wipes, a minimum of one change of clothes, and a burp cloth. If you want to use cloth diapers, remember to include a bag for transporting dirty or wet baby diapers at home, advise experts. Unless you are going somewhere where water safety isn't an issue, infant formula feeders must carry some bottles, solution, and water (for those using a powdery formula for liquid concentration). A second pacifier in your diaper bag might also be beneficial if your baby requires one. Some other valuables include a cleaning hand sanitizer, a pad, infant toys or novels, and clean clothing for a parent.

Where can my child sleep??

To facilitate frequent night feedings, placing newborns in the parent's room in cribs and bassinets is better. To avoid sudden infant death syndrome, your newborn should not go to sleep, and your bed should always rest lying back (SIDS).

You need to go to bed when the baby goes to sleep. Yes, your baby is lovely, and it's hard not to gaze at their face while your baby sleeps, but parents also need to sleep. Take a snooze yourself while the infant is asleep.

How Do I Swaddle a Baby?

Dad should find out from the nurses how to "swaddle" a newborn. In essence, a blanket is used to wrap an infant. It induces slumber in the infant by simulating the comfort of the womb.

How many car seats do I need?

To get the baby to and from the vehicle without waking them asleep, you first need an infant seat belt that clicks onto the base. Then, for the next several years, you'll need a car seat that can "convert" from facing backward to a forward-facing position.

Chapter 3: How to Support Your Partner During Labor

Although supporting your partner during labor might seem difficult and stressful, it is an important role that can affect how the labor and delivery process turns out. According to a study, a person in labor may benefit from ongoing assistance throughout delivery for themselves and the unborn child.

Labor might be a stressful event. Positive encouragement can shorten labor and enhance the result. Additionally, lending a hand may strengthen your relationship with your spouse as you tackle the difficulties of labor as a team. A person may feel less alone, safer, and more at ease if their partner is supportive and caring.

It is crucial to get as much advice and recommendations as you can if you are likely to be your wife's support person throughout labor and delivery so that you are ready to assist them. Everything you should know about helping your spouse during childbirth is provided here. Are you already wondering how to help your partner throughout labor and delivery? We gathered some guidance from seasoned parents and professionals who understand the inner workings to help you throughout the process.

3.1 Supporting Your Partner During Labor

Prepare for Labor and Delivery

Classes on birthing education can be a huge help in getting you ready for the future. Discover the stages of labor, what happened to your partner, and the justifications for a C-section. The encounter might be more comfortable for both of you if you know what to expect.

Even though work can be interesting, it can even be boring. Waiting alone could occupy hours of your time. Keep your spouse occupied to distract them from their discomfort. If your spouse receives an epidural, there might be less need for physical help in the early stages of labor. Instead, be prepared to engage her in the discussion, card games, and music.

Ask Questions

The delivery room is bustling with activity. Ask the doctor if anything is occurring that she doesn't understand again. Your partner's mind may also be at peace after hearing the response.

Show Your Support

During childbirth, one may experience panic. And their spouse is the ideal person to help them get their breathing back on track. You are the only one who knows them. Reassure your spouse that they are doing a fantastic job and that you love them when the contractions get more ferocious. Additionally, you can help by giving them ice chips or wiping the sweat from their forehead. Additionally, although some individuals prefer not to be touched when giving birth, others like receiving a shoulder or back massage; ask your spouse or the birthing nurse for advice if you need help with the best way to help them.

Monitor Contractions

While you can see the labor monitor, your spouse cannot. You can explain that you may talk to someone through contractions whenever the contractions peak and begin to subside. They may feel in charge by narrating what is taking place and when it begins and ends. (Remember that if they use an optical viewfinder, it only records the frequency of spasms, not their intensity.)

Get Pictures (With Permission)

Some angles work better for birth recordings than others. To put it another way, unless you never intend to reveal this tape to anybody else or you've discussed it beforehand, avoid pointing the camera directly at your partner's crotch. Naturally, there is nothing amiss with that viewpoint, but because it's their body, you'll want to ensure they agree.) You might videotape from the side or shoot over his wife's or the doctor's shoulder. Furthermore, ask your doctor or nurse about filming the delivery in advance since some don't allow it.

Advocate for Your Partner

Please do not wait until your spouse is experiencing agonizing contractions before asking what help they need. Find out in advance their birth plan, how they feel about episiotomies, and what they want from the doctor. Your spouse can decide to alter their mind due to the reality of childbirth.

On the other side, even if they've been having problems communicating, your spouse could require your assistance speaking out about what they want. More than anybody else in the room, you are familiar with them. Your responsibility is to stand behind your spouse, whatever they decide.

Don't Complain

Do not whine or look bored (no yawning). We often hear fathers lament having hurting backs from spending so much time standing close to their spouses. She continues by saying that the person giving birth is the only thing that matters during labor. During a contraction, a woman may desire to clutch her partner's hand.

Know That Giving Birth is Messy

Giving birth is messy, it's true! Even when pushing, your spouse can have a bowel movement. They'll most likely produce wild sounds you've not heard before. No matter how uneasy you may feel, it's your responsibility to tell the person, "You're doing fantastic!" They're again not listening to what you're saying. They are tuned in because of your recognizable voice and soothing tone. (Another disturbing detail is that the placenta, which must be released when the baby is born and resembles a large chunk of liver, must also be delivered.)

Make the Occasion Special

Your spouse is asleep, the infant is soundly dozing in the medical bassinet, and you have gotten in touch with the family. Both physically and mentally, your spouse has gone through a lot. It's a terrific opportunity to express your affection for her. Send her a love letter, buy her some expensive chocolates, or bring her favorite flowers. If you do go, find a unique method to commemorate the event.

Share Your Fears

Tell your doctor about your fears without holding back; even simply talking about them may be therapeutic, and she could have suggestions for calming you down. Consider seeking a new doctor if your current one lacks compassion or seems unwilling to listen.

Stay True to Yourself

Although labor changes you, it didn't help you fall in love with lime Jell-O, Postmodern music, or your in-laws at the sight of them as you endure a contraction. During work, others may try to convince you of all ideas; pay attention, but feel free to accept them.

Stick to your principles because it's you, your baby, and your labor. Think of it as a trial run for when your child is a teenager.

Don't personalize anything.

A laboring lady can be absorbed in her thoughts. Childbirth is a long, arduous process; some women discover that ignoring you and going within themselves is the finest way to cope. She could sometimes even show her irritation with you in public.

For instance, she could like massages in the early stages of labor but find them uncomfortable throughout the transition. And will be clear in letting you know that! The same is true for music; although the labor playlist you and she spent hours creating might have seemed like a terrific idea initially, she could eventually want complete stillness. (So, press pause.) It's crucial to avoid seeing any of her actions as a rejection of you.

Be a defender

It can be challenging for a woman giving birth to make difficult choices or adamant demands. Make sure you're prepared to intervene, if necessary, as her partner. You may need to assist her in weighing her alternatives rationally when it comes to specific medical issues. You might also request that her healthcare provider be roused from slumber, that an anesthetist is written up, or that a glass is brought in so she can glimpse what's going on.

Your doctor, midwife, and nurses are all there to ensure that your spouse and baby are healthy throughout labor and delivery. But you nonetheless play a significant position in assisting your spouse to feel comfortable and in conveying her needs. If she intends to breastfeed, ensure she gets the opportunity to do so as soon as the baby is delivered and that somebody is there to assist her if she needs it.

Pose inquiries to the medical personnel

Medical personnel must explain how they operate and if required, but they only sometimes do so. Be bold and ask questions, particularly if your spouse isn't capable of asking them herself, whether it's about medical practices, an update on how things are going, or how you might make your partner more comfortable.

It's common for silences to be unintentional, so don't be shy about speaking up. They're used to all kinds of questions. If you have any questions, the physicians, midwives, nurses, and perhaps other medical personnel will be pleased to respond, particularly if you attempt to provide the expectant mother with additional support.

Understand your limits

The birthing room is a very active place. It's critical to be conscious of your willingness to participate in the process and your desire to delegate some tasks to experts. For instance, if cutting the umbilical cord makes you uncomfortable (even if it was part of the original birth plan), say so.

Even though you didn't expect it, if the scene of carnage or even delivery makes you nauseous, realize that it's alright to turn your head. Don't feel embarrassed or humiliated. Instead, concentrate on your partner: Look her in the eyes and be there for her at this difficult time.

Pose inquiries to the medical personnel

Medical personnel must explain how they operate and if required, but they only sometimes do so. Be bold and ask questions, particularly if your spouse isn't capable of asking them herself, whether it's about medical practices, an update on how things are going, or how you might make your partner more comfortable.

Be there to provide support during labor and delivery

Simply being there is among the most crucial things to do for this significant life event. Even if you have to or prefer to leave most of the hands-on work to the medical professionals, your presence is still important. Your spouse will depend on you for support.

3.2 Packing Your Hospital Bag

If you're helping your wife prepare for labor and delivery, here are some items you may want to include in her hospital bag:

- Comfortable Clothing: Bring comfortable clothes for your wife to wear during labor and delivery, such as a loose-fitting nightgown or a nursing bra, as well as comfortable clothing to wear postpartum.

- Toiletries: Your wife may want to pack items such as a toothbrush, toothpaste, deodorant, shampoo, conditioner, and a hairbrush.

- Snacks: Pack snacks such as energy bars or dried fruit to energize your wife during labor and delivery.

- Massage Oil or Lotion: A massage can help your wife relax and ease her discomfort during labor, so consider bringing massage oil or lotion.

- Water Bottle: Staying hydrated during labor is essential, so bring a water bottle that your wife can refill throughout the day.

- Pillows and Blankets: Your wife may want to bring her own pillows or blankets from home to make the hospital room feel more comfortable and cozy.

- Entertainment: Bring a book, magazines, or other forms of entertainment to help your wife pass the time during early labor.

- Nursing Pads and Nipple Cream: These can help soothe sore nipples from breastfeeding.

- Phone and Charger: Your wife will want to keep her phone handy if she needs to make calls or take pictures.

- Comfort Items: Consider packing items to help your wife feel more comfortable, such as a heating pad, stress ball, or aromatherapy essential oils.

Remember, each hospital and labor experience may differ, so it's important to check with your healthcare provider about any additional items your wife should bring. And don't forget to pack some items for yourself, too, like a change of clothes, snacks, and a phone charger, as labor and delivery can be a long process.

3.3 Contractions and Labor

Your partner will start having contractions in the last month. Although contractions might be difficult to define, they often fit into any of the four types listed below.

Pre-Labor

Uterine Muscle spasms may start to get a bit stronger during the final few weeks of your pregnancy; there will be days when they are regular and arrive in groups of a few. The cervix is starting to soften in anticipation of actual labor.

Braxton Hicks

These movements are a normal part of getting ready for labor; they prepare the uterine fibers for such a big event and are often more frightening than unpleasant. In addition, they vary from other kinds of contractions in that their spacing is erratic.

False Labor

Your spouse may go through false labor if contractions begin as tightness in the upper stomach, become erratic over time, and finally cease.

True Labor

Your partner may be in labor if the surges are regular, rhythmic, painful, or unpleasant. Start timing the cramps at this point. The distance between the beginning of one and the beginning of the next, as well as their duration, should be noted. Your wife's doctor or obstetrician will tell you when to go to the hospital in the weeks before birth, for instance, when the contractions are out for at least a minute and are spaced out by 4 or 5 minutes.

3.4 Week-by-Week Pregnancy Advice

Pregnancy is different for partners than expectant mothers, but that doesn't mean it can't be a cooperative endeavor. While possibly suffering from morning, noon, and night sickness, you can still support your wife by giving her a calming smoothie. You won't be experiencing foot and back pain, but you may learn the technique of soothing her discomfort by giving her a foot and back massage. And even though you won't be giving delivery, you may be at her side encouraging and comforting her as she goes.

Put another way, you play a crucial role in the infant's development. For each week of the three trimesters, the following is what couples may anticipate.

First-trimester

Weeks 1 and 2

You may not notice many physical changes in her during the

first and second weeks of your wife's pregnancy. In fact, she may not even know she's pregnant at this early stage. During the first week, fertilization and implantation of the egg in the uterus occur. During the second week, the fertilized egg begins to divide and grow, and the placenta forms. However, your wife may experience some early pregnancy symptoms such as fatigue, mood swings, and breast tenderness. This is also a good time to start making healthy lifestyle changes, such as reducing alcohol and smoking and focusing on a well-balanced diet. It's important to offer your support and understanding during this time, as your wife may be feeling anxious or excited about the possibility of being pregnant.

Week 3

When sperm and egg combine, a single cell quickly divides into a minute mass. Those cells should eventually give rise to your baby in roughly nine months (plus or less).

You have yet to understand, so rather than trying to figure out what is taking place, try to put your thoughts elsewhere for the time being and allow nature to run its course. Locate a TV program where you can both lose yourselves (or laugh over).

Week 4

Give any bad habits a makeover while you and she attend her pregnancy test results before proceeding. Pregnancy advice for both men and women is as follows: If you smoke, give it up; secondhand smoke is detrimental to pregnant women's and newborns' health. Change them out for beneficial practices like taking brisk neighborhood walks after meals. In the next 36 weeks, both of you will be in better form.

Week 5

It's time to take prenatal testing right now. Your spouse may also be exhibiting early indicators, such as achy, sore breasts and the fracturing of bone weariness since the baby is now the width of an orange seed. Is there one task you can formally take over? If your cat has a litter box, clean it. Cat waste may carry parasites and spread the toxoplasmosis illness, which, while uncommon, might be harmful to pregnant women.

Week 6

Although the phrase "morning sickness" is a slang term deceptive since many expectant mothers experience nausea all day long, nausea might start right about now. Help ensure she has a nutritious snack (granola bar, trail mix) hidden on the bedside to munch depending on when she wakes up since an empty stomach might worsen nausea.

Keep short, simple-to-digest snacks like whole grain bread, almond butter, or hard cheddar cheese and crackers available if she struggles to consume large meals. Or learn how to make smoothies, which are equally simple on the abdominal region.

Week 7

At this stage, your partner's sensation of scent may be comparable to a bloodhound, so any offensive stench might cause her to immediately hurry to the restroom. If she claims your shoes smell after you take them off, it's time to stop wearing cologne-like perfume and accept her word for it. (Store them without making a sound.)

Week 8

Food aversions can increase in frequency for your spouse right now. If she cannot tolerate spinach or lettuce, substitute yellow vegetables like chilies or fruits such as mango, berries, and watermelon, all of which are rich in vitamins essential for the development of a baby.

Week 9

She is developing a mom's breasts and nipples, although they are presumably quite delicate. You may need to take it easy inside this bedroom since even the smallest touch can be too much.

Week 10

Up until birth, she will see the doctor for routine pregnancy exams. You should accompany her to certain appointments. You'll get a much-needed understanding of the extraordinary changes in her body by being present for her.

Your life will change forever when you hear the baby's first heartbeats. The best part is the opportunity to share those significant achievements with your wife. To grasp the doctors' orders and submit your questions, check if you can live telephone during the meeting if her doctor has a limit to the number of individuals who can visit the office.

Week 11

She needs to go now more often because of the hormones that cause kidney function to improve and urine to flow more often. When she wakes up three or four times throughout the night to go potty, you'll be acutely aware of this. Install nightlights inside the bathroom and hallway. Also, clear any obstacles to the bathroom to ensure your wife is safe.

Week 12

Some expectant mothers discover that the exhaustion, nausea, and bloating associated with pregnancy make them reluctant to engage in sexual activity. Find other techniques to get back together with your lover if they fit this description. You can surprise your partner by preparing tasty, sweet, and savory delicious snacks and meals. Staying in bed with a movie and some snacks is a far better option than going out.

Week 13

Sometimes partners may feel excluded from the pregnancy process, although this is natural. It's up to you to become involved if your spouse is talking about the baby with more than just her friends and relatives at this point in the first trimester since she likely has a lot on her mind (and a load and get off her chest). She may not even be aware that she is excluding you, or she could be reluctant to "run out" the subject so early in the pregnancy. By mentioning it yourself, you may put her at rest.

Second-trimester

Week 14

During week 14 of your wife's pregnancy, you can expect to see changes in her physical appearance as her belly grows. However, she may still have pregnancy symptoms such as backaches, headaches, and constipation. She may also experience increased energy as she feels less tired and nauseous. Your wife may also have an increased appetite and cravings for certain foods.

The fetus is developing rapidly, and at this stage, it is about 3.5 inches (8.9 cm) long and weighs about 1.5 ounces (43 grams). The baby's bones are beginning to harden, developing its facial features.

Your wife may have a prenatal check-up scheduled around this time, where the doctor will check the baby's growth and development and may also perform additional tests or screenings.

Week 15

During week 15 of your wife's pregnancy, you may notice that her belly grows as the baby develops. The baby is now about the size of an orange, around 4 inches (10 cm) long, and weighs about 2.5 ounces (70 grams).

Your wife may still experience pregnancy symptoms such as backaches, headaches, and constipation. She may also experience skin changes such as mild acne, darkening of the skin around her nipples, and a dark line down the middle of her belly (linea nigra). Still, she may feel more comfortable in her clothing as her body adjusts to the changes.

Your wife's appetite may continue to increase, and she may crave certain foods. She needs to continue to eat a healthy, balanced diet and stay hydrated.

Your wife may have a prenatal check-up scheduled during this time, where the doctor will monitor the baby's growth and development, check her blood pressure, and may perform additional tests or screenings.

It's important to provide your wife with emotional support during this time, as she may feel a range of emotions about the pregnancy and the changes happening to her body.

Week 16

During week 16 of your wife's pregnancy, you can expect the baby to continue growing rapidly. At this stage, the baby is about the size of an avocado, approximately 4.6 inches (11.6 cm) in length, and weighs around 3.5 ounces (100 grams).

One interesting development during this week is that your wife may start to feel more pronounced movements from the baby as it becomes more active. Although these movements may still be subtle, they can be a source of great joy and excitement for both you and your wife.

While your wife may experience some pregnancy symptoms such as backaches, headaches, and constipation, her appetite may continue increasing, and she may crave certain foods. She needs to continue to eat a healthy, balanced diet and stay hydrated.

As your wife's uterus expands, it may put pressure on her bladder and cause her to urinate more frequently. This is normal and will continue throughout the pregnancy.

Your wife's prenatal check-ups will continue, and the doctor will monitor the baby's growth and development, check her blood pressure, and may perform additional tests or screenings. It's important to attend these appointments with your wife and ask any questions you may have.

It's important to continue providing emotional support to your wife. Pregnancy can be an emotional rollercoaster, and your wife may experience a range of emotions as her body undergoes significant changes.

Week 17

Pregnancy hormones stuff the unknown in Your partner's nose, and one of the side effects may be snoring while sleeping. It's just temporary, so don't worry.

If it keeps you awake at night, consider installing a mister in the room to help her breathe easier (plus, you can apply it in the nursery when the baby is a few months old). Alternatively, spend additional money on pillows so she may sleep with her head up.

Week 18

You're the greatest partner you can be, but one of the ways you achieve that is by taking on the role of cook more often than normal. (Bringing in takeout counts if you don't want to cook.)

Think quickly, simply, and easily. What's on your menu during pregnancy is just as significant as what's off. For the immediate being, avoid rare steaks, Caesar salad, raw fish sushi, and seared fish since they are all off-limits. Avoid anything too spicy or fatty to prevent heartburn. She could eat four times a day, so supper can be easy. An earlier meal hour could also be welcomed if she has been exhausted or is experiencing heartburn.

Week 19

Are you getting teary-eyed when you see infant onesies? It's your hormones' fault. Yes, during your wife's pregnancy, you might experience a decrease in testosterone and an increase in estrogen. Nature does this to keep you close to home and to put you in a caring mindset so you can take care of your child.

What do you do in this regard? Nothing. Just know that your progesterone levels will likely return to normal within about six months, just after the baby is delivered. Just follow along for the time being.

Week 20

Week 20 of your wife's pregnancy is a major milestone in the journey toward parenthood. At this point, the baby is about the size of a banana, measuring around 6.5 inches (16.5 cm) in length and weighing approximately 10.6 ounces (300 grams). This means that your wife's belly is likely to be much more noticeable, and strangers may start to notice and comment on her pregnancy.

One of the most exciting developments during this week is that your wife will have her second-trimester ultrasound, which is also known as the anatomy scan. This detailed scan will check the baby's growth and development, including the major organs, limbs, and brain. This is an exciting opportunity for both you and your wife to see the baby for the first time, and the ultrasound technician may even be able to tell you the gender of the baby (if you choose to find out).

Your wife may continue to experience some pregnancy symptoms such as fatigue, backaches, and constipation. However, as she reaches the halfway point of her pregnancy, she may start to feel more energized and less nauseous than she did in the first trimester.

As the baby keeps growing, your wife's uterus will also expand, putting pressure on her organs and causing her to feel more discomfort. She may experience shortness of breath or heartburn due to the baby pushing up on her diaphragm and stomach. She needs to take breaks when she needs to and prioritize rest and self-care.

As the due date approaches, it's important to start thinking about preparing for the baby's arrival. This could include setting up the nursery, buying baby gear such as a stroller or car seat, and researching childbirth classes or breastfeeding resources.

Overall, week 20 of your wife's pregnancy is an exciting time full of new developments and preparations for the arrival of your little one. Enjoy this time with your wife.

Week 21

Congratulations, you've made it to week 21 of your wife's pregnancy! At this point, your baby is approximately the size of a carrot, weighing around 12.7 ounces and measuring about 10.5 inches from head to toe. As your baby grows and develops, you can expect some exciting changes and developments during this week.

One of the most exciting changes during week 21 is the development of your baby's digestive system. Your baby's intestines are now forming meconium, the first stool your baby will pass after birth. Additionally, your baby's taste buds are now developing, which means that he or she can start to distinguish different tastes in the amniotic fluid.

Another exciting development during week 21 is the development of your baby's sense of touch. Your baby's skin is becoming more sensitive, and he or she can now feel pressure and respond to touch. This means that if you place your hand on your wife's belly, your baby may be able to feel your touch and respond with a kick or movement.

As your baby continues to grow, your wife may start to experience some new pregnancy symptoms during week 21. For example, she may notice that she is feeling more tired or fatigued, as her body is working hard to support the growing baby. She may also experience some mild swelling in her hands or feet, which is a common symptom of pregnancy.

Week 22

Are you worried that having sex would injure the baby? There's nothing to worry about! Enjoy yourself, as your partner's doctor has gotten her the all-clear. In the womb, where it is safe, your baby is unable to see or hear what is happening. You may need to experiment with positions that accommodate her tummy, but that's OK; you could discover a novel method to express your love.

Week 23

Welcome to week 23 of your wife's pregnancy! At this point, your baby is growing rapidly and is now approximately the size of a grapefruit, measuring around 11.4 inches from head to toe and weighing in at just over a pound. As your baby develops, you can expect to see some exciting changes and developments this week.

One of the most significant developments during week 23 is the formation of your baby's lungs. At this stage, your baby's lungs are beginning to produce a substance called surfactant, which helps the lungs to expand and contract properly after birth. This is an important step in your baby's development, as it helps to prepare your baby for life outside of the womb.

Another exciting development during week 23 is the development of your baby's hearing. Your baby's ears are now fully formed, and he or she can hear sounds inside and outside the womb. This means that your baby can now hear your voice and the sound of your heartbeat and may even respond with a kick or movement.

As your baby continues to grow, your wife may start to experience some new symptoms during week 23. For example, she may notice that she feels more fatigued as her body works hard to support the growing baby. She may also experience some mild shortness of breath as her growing uterus puts pressure on her diaphragm.

Week 24

Yes! You've made it to week 24 of your wife's pregnancy! At this stage, your baby is the size of an ear of corn, measuring around 12.6 inches from head to toe and weighing in at around 1.3 pounds. You can expect to see exciting changes and developments at this stage.

One of the most significant developments during week 24 is your baby's brain's continued growth and maturation. Your baby's brain is growing rapidly, and the nerve cells are now forming the connections necessary for brain function. This means that your baby can now respond to more complex stimuli and even start dreaming!

Another exciting development during week 24 is the growth of your baby's taste buds. Your baby's sense of taste is now developing, and he or she can taste the different flavors of the amniotic fluid. This means that what your wife eats can influence your baby's developing palate, so it's important for her to eat a healthy and varied diet.

Your wife may start to experience some new pregnancy symptoms during week 24. For example, she may notice that her skin is becoming more sensitive, and she may develop stretch marks as her belly expands. She may also experience mild back pain as her growing uterus puts pressure on her lower back.

Week 25

It's week 25 of your wife's pregnancy, a truly exciting time as you're now officially in the second half of your pregnancy journey! At this stage, your baby is about the size of a cauliflower, measuring around 13.6 inches from head to toe and weighing in at around 1.5 pounds. There are some amazing changes and milestones to look forward to this week.

One of the most significant developments during week 25 is the maturation of your baby's lungs. This is a crucial milestone, as it means your baby is now much more likely to survive if he or she is born prematurely. Your baby's lungs are now producing a substance called surfactant, which helps them to expand and contract properly after birth.

Another exciting development during week 25 is the continued growth of your baby's taste buds. Your baby's sense of taste is now developing, and he or she can taste the different flavors of the amniotic fluid. This means that what your wife eats can influence your baby's developing palate, so it's important for her to eat a healthy and varied diet.

As your baby continues to grow, your wife may start to experience some new pregnancy symptoms during week 25. For example, she may notice that her belly is growing at a faster pace, which can lead to stretch marks and skin irritation. She may also experience mild Braxton Hicks contractions, which are a normal part of pregnancy but can be uncomfortable.

Remember that your wife may experience some or all of these symptoms, or she may not experience any at all.

Week 26

You should expect to see more signs of progress from the baby throughout this 26th week of her pregnancy. Baby is about 14 inches long from head to toe and weighs around 1.7 pounds at this point, making him or her roughly the size of a head of lettuce.

The eyes of your baby continue to develop at a rapid pace throughout this 26th week. Your newborn's eyes are fully developed at this point, allowing your child to blink and even move them. Your infant may be more alert or sleepy at specific times of the day as sleep and waking cycles become more regular.

Your wife's symptoms during pregnancy may change during week 26 as the baby develops further. As her tummy expands, she can feel discomfort in her back and legs, and her feet and ankles might swell. Rest and self-care are all that is needed to alleviate these common symptoms.

Week 27

As your wife's bulge grows, the skin enlarges, dries up, and gets itchier. Scratching won't bring her any solace. So, take charge and slather shea butter or moisturizer over her stomach. It's a soothing way to interact with your friend.

Third-trimester

Week 28

As your wife enters week 28 of her pregnancy, you may notice her physical discomforts and emotional ups and downs are becoming more pronounced. This is a crucial time for you to step up and help her as much as possible. Here are some ways you can support your wife during this important phase:

Attend prenatal appointments with her: Make sure you accompany your wife to her prenatal checkups. Ask questions and take an active role in her healthcare. It will make her feel more supported and cared for.

Help her manage her stress: As the pregnancy progresses, your wife may experience more stress and anxiety. Encourage her to practice relaxation techniques like deep breathing and meditation. Plan some fun activities together to help her unwind.

Provide emotional support: Your wife may feel a wide range of emotions, from excitement to fear, as the due date approaches. Be there to listen and validate her feelings. Offer encouragement and let her know you're there for her no matter what.

Help her with household tasks: Your wife may find it challenging to keep up with the household chores during this time. Offer to help with cooking, cleaning, laundry, and other tasks to lighten her load.

Encourage healthy habits: Eating well and exercising regularly can help your wife stay healthy during pregnancy. Encourage her to eat a balanced diet and exercise safely for her and the baby.

By supporting your wife during week 28 and throughout her pregnancy, you can help her stay healthy, happy, and confident as she prepares to welcome your new baby into the world.

Week 29

Week 29 of your wife's pregnancy is a time of significant changes for both your baby and your wife. Your baby is growing rapidly and becoming more active, so your wife may feel more fetal movements. She may also experience Braxton Hicks contractions, shortness of breath, swelling in her hands, feet, and ankles, and increased fatigue. While these changes can be uncomfortable, they are normal and can be managed with rest, relaxation techniques, and self-care. Encourage your wife to take care of herself and seek advice from her healthcare provider if she has any concerns.

Week 30

During week 30 of your wife's pregnancy, your baby continues to grow and develop, and your wife may experience various physical and emotional changes. Your baby is now about the size of a cabbage and may weigh up to 3 pounds. Your wife's uterus is expanding, which can cause discomfort, and she may experience more frequent Braxton Hicks contractions. She may also have trouble sleeping due to the baby's movements and the pressure on her bladder. Emotionally, your wife may feel more anxious or stressed as the reality of impending parenthood sets in. This is a good time to provide support and reassurance and help your wife practice self-care to manage any physical or emotional discomforts.

Week 31

Pregnancy's cognitive impairment also makes things worse). This week, your baby has grown to the amount of a coconut, which is harder for your partner's body. She needs to change her posture to make room for that expanding tummy, which can make her clumsier.

Install a doorknob on the bathroom mirror and roll up dark colors (or tape him down) right away so she can easily enter and exit the shower.

Week 32

Quick! How recently have you seen your primary care physician? If you can't recall, it's time to make an office or, at the very least, give your doctor a call to check on your vaccination status.

This is why: You must safeguard your newborn from diseases like the flu & severe cough (often known as bronchitis), which may harm babies after birth. Another interesting fact is that most babies get whooping cough from family members.

You most likely had a Tdap vaccination as a child, but you now need a booster. Additionally, getting your annual flu vaccination, often available in September, is always crucial. So, make a visiting appointment and dig up your sleeves. Baby will appreciate it.

Week 33

It's time for two to go doctor shopping while you're booking your appointment. Check with your network of nearby new or soon-to-be parents to see if they can suggest any regional doctors. Read the reviews of surrounding physicians by searching Google. Alternatively, request the names of your suppliers.

Then, create a series of questions after confirming if they accept your insurance. You should enquire about their approach to patient care, level of experience, hours of operation, and if you can reach them after hours, among other things.

Week 34

It's time for everyone to put together the hospital overnight bag. Check if she has everything in the suitcase and discusses the personal things she wants to bring. She undoubtedly understands what she takes, but with the excitement and worry you both may be experiencing, she can forget something.

Carry a change of clothing for yourself and any toiletries you may need if you expect to spend more than 24 hours at the airport or birthing facility. Don't forget to bring food, a phone charger, and maybe a computer with films and games if labor is protracted and you both need to be distracted.

Week 35

It may have already occurred to you that your child's delivery could be among those sensational roadside births in the backseat with a traffic officer there and reported on by the 10 o'clock news. Even if it is unlikely, be ready for that eventuality, and remember that there are things you can do to lessen the likelihood that it will occur.

Given the unpredictable nature of traffic patterns and roving construction personnel, doing a test run is not a terrible idea. Aside from having the several routes to the hospital or birthing facility stored on your phone, ensure the vehicle has petrol. Additionally, it wouldn't hurt to put a blanket, a liter of bottled water, and some towels in the backseat only in case.

Week 36

Your kid would be premature if she opted to give birth this week. So, if you haven't already, consider the following wonderful partner pregnancy advice: Discuss something with your supervisor. If you often travel for business, you can remark that you need to stay near your home for a bit. And if your wife gives birth while you work, you'd appreciate the freedom to leave without much notice.

Your supervisor probably appreciates the unpredictable nature of everything and can sympathize. Additionally, if you haven't done, you should apply for any maternity and paternity leave they want to take.

Week 37

It's funny how you never noticed how crowded your closet was until you decided to arrange it. And that cupboard over there has to be cleaned out immediately. Not to consider the cellar Congratulations, your nesting urge has shown itself (yes, non-pregnant spouses may also feel it).

Don't be shocked if you suddenly have the motivation to do obsessive painting, cleaning, and organizing. Run with it (and with the dust); it's nature's way of ensuring that your baby will have a cozy, clean nest when you all get home. Additionally, it distracts you from your pre-delivery anxiety at this point.

Even if your wife could be going into nesting overdrive, don't allow her. Alternatively, her current instinct may be one of exhaustion.

Week 38

You both can be in the desire for sex but are unsure whether it will start labor. Go through the plan if her practitioner hasn't expressly disapproved of it. You have the option to complete the action.

Week 39

During week 39 of your wife's pregnancy, your baby is considered full-term and ready to be born at any time. Your baby's size and weight have likely stabilized, and they are now around 20 inches long and can weigh up to 7.5 pounds. At this point, the baby's organs, including the lungs and digestive system, are fully developed and functioning, meaning they can breathe and digest independently.

Your wife may experience some physical discomfort during week 39, such as back pain, fatigue, and difficulty sleeping. As the baby drops lower into the pelvis, your wife may feel more pressure on her bladder, which can result in more frequent urination. She may also experience Braxton Hicks contractions, which are mild contractions that help prepare the uterus for labor.

Your healthcare provider will likely want to see your wife for more frequent prenatal checkups during week 39 to monitor the baby's position, heartbeat, and overall health. They will also check your wife's cervix for signs of dilation and effacement, which are indications that labor is approaching.

Week 39 of pregnancy marks an exciting time as you and your wife prepare to welcome your little one into the world. It's essential to stay in close communication with your healthcare provider and be prepared for the unexpected, as labor can happen at any time.

Week 40

Your spouse may be one of the roughly one-third of expecting women who go 40 weeks or more and achieve full term. If so, be cool and collected so that you may assist her in calming down.

To avoid those bothersome calls to ask if there's any news, you could also wish to SMS your friends and relatives. When your kid begins to make her entrance known, assure them you'll be in contact immediately.

Additional methods to assist: If you haven't already, install the car seat, hang the motion and the nightlights in the nursery, then wash and hang all of the precious baby clothes. Additionally, you may prepare some simple frozen recipes (such as turkey meatballs, vegetarian chili, chicken soups, and muffins) to make your life simpler once the baby is born.

Week 41

According to research, 96 percent of women are ready to attempt nursing when fathers support it (as opposed to 26 halves when dads aren't too into it). Be your partner's champion and request a nurse-expert lactation consultant to swing by and advise if she's chosen to breastfeed after the baby is delivered and before two leave the hospital.

When you go home, take the infant to her for breastfeeding and ensure she has access to food and drink. It takes effort to breastfeed.

Week 42

Although you may believe your baby is beyond due, due dates are just estimations and might vary for another week or two. Your partner's doctor keeps an eye on things to ensure everything is OK inside, even if your baby is OK.

Utilize this additional week to stock up on cupboard and refrigerator necessities, such as paper products and straightforward foods. Additionally, get diapers and other necessities for your newborn baby while shopping. After completing all of that, relax and anticipate the big day. Now, not much longer.

Chapter 4: Guide for Expectant Fathers for Trimesters

Many parents-to-be are unclear about what to expect when their partner approaches the third trimester or from the 28th week of pregnancy until delivery. Although it may seem like these last few weeks are moving slowly, your baby is really growing rapidly, which may cause your partner's belly to enlarge and hurt.

Well, the last stages of your pregnancy are a key period for preparation as you and your spouse eagerly await the arrival of your kid. You should begin preparing for your child's birth and assist your partner in any way possible. By 32 weeks, your child is fully formed, if a bit slender. In the next weeks, the lungs will grow, and newborn males' testicles will move into the scrotum. By the end of the third trimester, they will be around 6 and 9 pounds as well as 19 and 21 inches long. At about 36 weeks, their head may come into contact with or sink toward the pelvic area in anticipation of birth. This "lightning" method should provide your buddy some comfort. Let's look at what you, your partner, and your child might anticipate throughout the third trimester and how to prepare.

Most people experience some degree of discomfort and fatigue as their child develops. The weight and much more active motion of your baby might cause a number of health problems for your partner, including a hurting back, restlessness, and sleeplessness. Support, thoughtfulness, and compassion might be helpful during this time.

Due to the body temperature increase caused by your baby's heat radiation, your spouse may have frequent episodes of heat exhaustion. Additionally, individuals may need to go to the bathroom more often since their bladders are working harder. People may also have edema in their limbs, ankles, and faces as a result of fluid retention.

4.1 A Partner's Guide to the First Trimester

Congratulations if your spouse is going to become a parent. It may be both thrilling and overwhelming during this time, but knowing what to expect will help you be ready for the baby's birth. Additionally, it might help you be there for your partner when she experiences a range of physical and emotional changes.

The First Trimester

A woman's uterus expands during the first few weeks of pregnancy, going from the capacity of a tangerine to the dimensions of a small melon.

Maternal Physical and Emotional Changes

Even when the uterus is still very tiny at this point, women may start to develop a little pooch. In addition, a lot of women have cramping, which is a bit of a misnomer since it may last all day.

Shifts in hormone levels may cause emotional changes in women. Recognize that this is typical and provide your assistance so she can get through challenging times. You two must communicate well with one another. It is beneficial to discuss any issues or concerns you may have with a family friend or member of your family.

Fetal Growth

The fetus develops from an unobservable fertilized cell to a recognizable creature with emerging traits. The mouth, lips, and eyes are appropriately formed, and the face is created. The external ears are noticeable. By the fourteenth week, the infant's sex is clear, and the specific anatomical organs have grown and matured. Even though the lungs, liver, intestines, and gut still need to develop and expand, the testicles are now completely developed.

Having Sex in the First Trimester

Having sex during the first trimester of your wife's pregnancy is generally safe and healthy for both your wife and the developing fetus. However, it's always a good idea to talk to your healthcare provider about any concerns or questions you may have.

During the first trimester, your wife's body is undergoing significant changes, and some women may experience vaginal bleeding or spotting. In this case, it's best to avoid having sex and consult with your healthcare provider.

Otherwise, you can continue to have sex as long as your wife is comfortable and there are no complications with the pregnancy. Some positions may be more comfortable than others as your wife's body changes, and you may need to experiment to find what works best for both of you.

It's essential to communicate openly with your partner about any discomfort or concerns during sex and to be patient and gentle with each other. Remember that the baby is well-protected by the amniotic sac and the cervix, and it is highly unlikely that sex will harm the baby.

If your wife has a history of miscarriage or is at risk of preterm labor, your healthcare provider may recommend avoiding sex or limiting sexual activity during the first trimester. In general, it's always best to consult with your healthcare provider to ensure that sex is safe and healthy for both your wife and the developing fetus.

Prenatal Care

Several medical appointments, testing, and waiting for outcomes throughout pregnancy occur. Support is one of your main responsibilities at this time. Attending visits will support

your spouse and help you learn about your baby's growth and development.

You may see the baby's growth via ultrasound scans. The first time you get to view the small fetus is a fantastic experience. This test and others may assist in establishing your kid's safety and reveal any anomalies. Additional testing might include:

- **Glucose Tolerance Testing**

This quick blood test checks to determine whether the patient has a gem, a type of diabetes that develops during pregnancy.

- **Amniocentesis**

This test may aid in genetic problems and prenatal lung maturity screening.

- **AFP**

A screening tool for neural tube abnormalities is called AFP. It often occurs in conjunction with other indicators being measured in order to determine the risk of down syndrome

- **Chorionic Villus Sampling (CVS)**

This genetic disease test is conducted between ten and twelve weeks of pregnancy.

4.2 How Partners Can Prepare for Baby's Arrival

You may be better prepared by getting ready for your child's birth and helping your spouse in the following months. Here are some things to think about:

Take Care of Yourself

But remember to look after your health, especially by getting enough sleep. A balanced diet, plenty of sleep, and exercise help you manage your stress and become a better companion. Even though you won't be the one in childbirth, you still need to be prepared to assist and soothe your spouse throughout the whole labor and delivery process.

Support Your Partner

Ask about what they can do to help your spouse through these last several months, and then do it. They may need assistance with last-minute preparations for the baby, such as completing the nursery or buying supplies. Consider doing additional housework so that they relax or have snacks and meals prepared for them. Supporting your spouse may be as simple as giving them a back massage or doing tiny things for them to help them relax and unwind.

Prepare for Labor and Delivery

You can help create a birthing plan with your spouse. Learn the labor symptoms so you can recognize when it is time to visit the hospital. This might help you feel included in the process and also inform you of your partner's preferences. Participating in this process gives you a sense of what to expect, what you'll see, and how best to assist your spouse throughout labor.

You may also view birth-related films at your leisure or at childbirth education programs. Observing a range of deliveries could make you more prepared for anything. Recognizing that labor and delivery may go differently than planned is also crucial.

Pack for the Hospital

Not only you and your spouse will need luggage for the hospital. Additionally, it would help if you had a backpack packed with a change of clothing, toiletries, and a sleeping bag at the ready.

Think about bringing some small food, cash for the machines, and a cord for charging your phone. If your phone dies or your GPS malfunctions as labor begins, you should bring paper instructions for going to the hospital.

Install the Car Seat

You are obliged to put a car seat in your vehicle to transport your newborn home from the hospital. Early installation of the car seat offers you time to ensure appropriate installation. You should still have it examined as an extra precaution.

Spend Quality Time Together

Before the infant turns three, cherish and strengthen the link you already have before your relationship undergoes a significant transformation. Enjoy the last weeks before the birth of your child with your spouse. Take strolls together and linger over a tasty meal. Watch a favorite TV or movie while cuddling up on the sofa. The most important thing is to spend some peaceful time before the baby is born.

It's common to have prenatal anxiety and worry about the delivery and how that will affect your spouse and the unborn child. Remember that many people carry a baby every day, even though it often seems stressful or frightening, and that for many couples, having children is one of life's greatest pleasures.

Speak to your spouse if you need help adjusting to these upcoming changes. Working together and coming up with ideas need effective communication. But most importantly, give yourself space to savor the prospect of being a parent.

Talk About Your Concerns

And during late pregnancy, communication is essential, so if you have worries about the delivery or the wellness of your baby, speak to your boyfriend, friends, family, and friends, or a healthcare professional to receive the answers you need. Receiving assistance from others may improve your ability to support your spouse in the best way possible.

4.3 A Partner's Guide to Pregnancy in the Third Trimester

Many soon-to-be parents are unsure what to anticipate as their spouse enters the third trimester or from around the 28th week through pregnancy to birth. While it may feel like these last few weeks are passing slowly, your baby is developing quickly, which might make your partner's tummy grow bigger and cause some pain.

As you and your partner anxiously anticipate your child's birth, well, the last weeks of your pregnancy are a crucial time for preparation. In addition to starting to get ready for your kid's birth, you'll want to help your spouse in any capacity possible. Let's examine what to expect throughout the third trimester for you, your spouse, and your kid and how to get ready.

Baby's Third Trimester Development

During these last several months, your baby's growth will

undergo a lot of change. Your baby's growth and weight continue to grow throughout this time. While their lungs, kidneys, and intellect are still growing, they can see and hear.

Your child will now be coated in vernix, a greasy material that shields them first from the intrauterine fluid surrounding growing in the womb when her companion is 28 weeks pregnant. In addition, the size of your genital region has increased to match that of your head. And should they be born prematurely, they may now survive with specialist care.

Your kid is completely developed by 32 weeks, although a little skinny. The lungs will develop during the next weeks, and the testicles of male newborns will slide into the scrotum. They will be between 6 and 9 pounds and 19 and 21 inches long by the completion of the third trimester. In preparation for delivery, their head may interact with or dip into the pelvic region at about 36 weeks. This procedure, known as "lightning," ought to provide solace for your companion.

4.4 Pregnant Parent's Experience

Most individuals feel a fair degree of pain and weariness as their baby grows. The spouse may experience various physical issues due to your baby's weight and more active movements, such as sore back, restlessness, and insomnia. Showing support, consideration, and compassion may make a difference during this time.

Your spouse could have frequent bouts of heat exhaustion due to your baby's heat radiation raising their body temperature. Additionally, since their bladders are under greater strain, they may be required to use the toilet more often. Additionally, due to fluid retention, people may have edema in their limbs, ankles, and faces.

Additionally, it's possible that throughout this time, they lose interest in having sex. Additionally, they could have more frequent heartburn, indigestion, and constipation, making them feel worse. Moreover, when they get closer to giving birth, they could suffer Braxton-Hicks contractions, often known as false labor. Being sympathetic to all the things they are going through and offering to soothe them is the finest thing anyone can do.

4.5 How to Help Your Partner Through the Last Month of Pregnancy

There's no denying that being pregnant can be a thrilling yet perplexing moment for you and your spouse. If you have survived the first eight weeks, you have undoubtedly already experienced cravings, mood swings, severe sickness, new sexual encounters, and other things. This still falls short of adequately preparing you for the last month of your partner's pregnancy. The last month when pregnancy brings a new range of feelings and discomforts.

Here, we examine what to anticipate and your partner's potential emotions so that you may effectively assist them and go through the third month of your pregnancy together.

4.6 What to Expect in the Last Month of Pregnancy

The last phase of pregnancy may bring a variety of physical obstacles as well as a variety of emotions, from relief to dread. Comprehending their possible physical and emotional states to accompany your spouse during this last phase is essential.

Listed below are some things you need to be aware of about your partner's possible pregnancy-related experiences in the last month.

Exhaustion

The body is now working overtime. Your spouse will often experience exhaustion as the baby grows and uses more energy.

Feeling Uncomfortable

The baby continues to develop and changes positions throughout the final month of pregnancy. Your companion could have abdominal pain. Because of the tightened skin, maternity clothing, too, won't fit. This could make your spouse feel inadequate, uneasy, or disheartened.

Moving

Every movement of your chosen partner will seem difficult due to the baby's size and location. It might be challenging to

emerge from a chair, get into bed, or even move to the restroom.

Bathroom Runs

After the pregnancy, the baby starts to exert increased pressure on the bladder, necessitating more toilet visits from your spouse. When leaving home, particularly, have a strategy in place.

Mood Swings

Be prepared for a range of emotions from your spouse. They may sometimes display excitement and devotion. They may also feel unhappy, exhausted, irritable, and impatient at other times. Be kind and patient with your spouse while they experience these ups and downs.

Anxiety

Assist your spouse in preparing the home for the newborn and soothe their fears about money, family, becoming a new mother, and other issues. As a result of such knowledge, cleanliness (the "nesting instinct") may occur. Between you and your spouse, the imminent delivery is becoming a reality.

Just Be There

There may be moments when there won't be much you can accomplish to cheer up your spouse. You may give them a gentle embrace, foot massage, or lower back rub. The procedure will go more smoothly if you pay attention to and address your partner's demands.

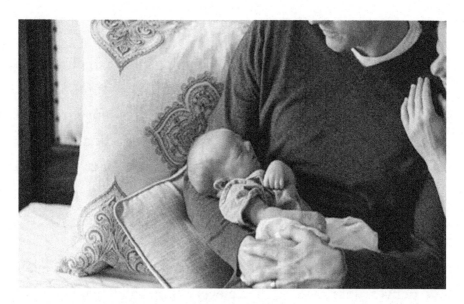

Supporting Your Partner

Fortunately, you may react to your spouse's emotions by going along with them, providing comfort, and being compassionate. Your wife may sometimes want to converse and cuddle, while other times, they may want some distance.

Please do not attempt to push your perspective on your relationship; rather, take your partner's lead in learning about their preferences. Putting pain or rejection aside is crucial since the necessary space isn't personal.

Keep It Simple

Keep things simple and actively engaged the whole time your spouse is expecting. Start by lowering the standards for meals, housework, and other distractions. You may also prepare meals in advance to reheat later.

4.7 Visit the Doctor Together

Taking your wife to the doctor and keeping tabs on their growth is another opportunity to be engaged in this beautiful process. You should be ready to accompany her at her more frequent obstetrician appointments throughout the final month. Additionally, this is a chance for you to ask crucial medical questions.

4.8 Preparation for the Hospital

A little pre-labor anxiety may be reduced by having your labor and delivery kit prepared. Bring everything you'll need for your hospital visit in your baggage, including:

- **Overnight bag**: Pajamas, toiletries (such as toothpaste, toothpaste, brush, deodorant, etc.), a change of clothing, a nursing bra, and other items may be in your partner's overnight bag.

- **Car seat**: You must comply with this crucial safety requirement to bring the infant home. Installing this car seat ahead of time ensures correct installation (and possibly even getting it tested) and crosses one item off your preparation list.

- **Light snacks**: A refreshing change from what the hospital offers may be found in little cans of orange juice, crackers, and raisins. Sandwiches, bananas, and energy bars are also acceptable additions. However, many medical professionals advise avoiding consuming any solid meals during childbirth.

- **Camera**: You'll be happy to have it on hand when the baby is born for your first family photo.

- **Music**: Many mothers appreciate relaxing music during labor and when their baby is delivered.

- **Money**: It's a good idea to have cash or a credit card on board for unforeseen expenses, such as meals, parking, and other things.

- **Comfort items**: Ensure adequate massage supplies, such as cold or hot packs, since these may be quite effective at relieving pain.

- **Electronics**: Bring your cell, charger, and other necessities, such as an address book, so you may contact your loved ones right when you leave the hospital.

- **Hospital route**: Make sure your GPS is configured for the route to the hospital. Jotting down the directions beforehand can provide peace of mind and ensure a timely arrival at the hospital. However, it's also wise to have a backup plan in case of GPS malfunction.

Chapter 5: How to Facilitate Labor and the Time Afterwards

You may be interested in the outcomes if you visit a hospital or birthing facility and pretend to be in labor but are instead sent home. When you arrive at the hospital or birthing facility where you will give birth, a nurse will often welcome you and help you settle in, determining whether or not a woman is indeed in labor before moving on. This can need some time spent watching. This often entails monitoring the baby's activity level, the rhythm, intensity, and response of the contractions on the cervix.

Even though the instant your baby is born and the moments that follow may be tremendously important to you, a lot usually happens during this time. The way your kid was delivered, as well as your partner's and your child's health, will all affect what happens in the minutes immediately after the birth of your child.

You and your wife may find it useful to talk about how the new baby should be cared for during the first few hours of life. We have wonderful news for expectant parents: planning for yet another milestone "moon" is something you can look forward to. It makes no difference whether you are a first-time parent or an experienced parent. It's a good chance to rekindle your relationship with your spouse and build your connection as a couple tasked with parenting children during that little window of time before your family expands. A babymoon is a brief trip or vacation done by a couple just before the birth of their kid.

5.1 Being Sent Home from the Hospital When Not in Labor

You may have learned about fake labor at your birthing class, through friends and family, or both. The phrase "false labor" is a little misleading since countless people would interpret it as meaning that false labor symptoms are neither painful nor fruitful. You may have one of these, but still, you need to be while in labor.

Being a mother may be stressful, especially toward the end of the pregnancy (no pun intended). Inconvenient indications and symptoms that make life more difficult to handle in certain ways start to appear during the last weeks of pregnancy. The worst scenario is when these signs are misdiagnosed as labor.

Premature hospital visits

You may be curious about what results you can expect if you go to the medical center or the birthing facility and claim to be in labor but are instead sent home. A nurse will often greet you when you get to the place, the airport or birth center, where you will give birth, and assist you in settling in. Determining whether or not currently in actual labor to step in this procedure. This can entail a time of observation. This often involves keeping an eye on the baby's energy levels, contractions pattern, severity, and how one's cervix reacts to them.

This procedure is finished during the triage section of several hospitals. In most hospitals, this ward has beds divided by drapes or close to the floor designated for labor and delivery in extremely tiny rooms. Usually, you will be quizzed and have a short time monitoring the fetus. After that, your cervix will be examined.

5.2 When Can You Expect to Be Admitted to The Hospital to Begin Your Labor?

The timing of when a woman and her partner can expect to be admitted to the hospital for labor can vary depending on a variety of factors, including the individual woman's medical history and the progress of her labor. In general, most women are admitted to the hospital when they are in active labor and have reached a certain level of cervical dilation, which is typically around 4-6 centimeters.

However, some women may be admitted earlier if there are concerns about the health of the mother or baby or if they are experiencing complications.

On the other hand, some women may be advised to wait longer before going to the hospital if they are having a low-risk pregnancy and are not experiencing strong contractions.

Ultimately, the decision about when to go to the hospital should be made in consultation with a healthcare provider, who can offer personalized guidance based on the woman's individual circumstances.

5.3 Consequences of Jumping the Gun Too Soon

Several people believe that going to the doctor or hospital would speed up labor. The opposite is not always the case true. In fact, it is not true that most pregnant women, especially those with less risky conception, should just sit in the hospital waiting for their labor to progress. According to research, women who are sent to the doctor or hospital extremely early in their labor may face more risks and need more intervention compared to those who stay at home and observe labor until they progress naturally.

This perfectly illustrates when you arrive in the hospital early while in labor. You may remain within the hospital, utilize Pitocin or artificially rupture your water to start labor more quickly, or you can go home and wait. These final two factors may raise the risk of difficulties for both you and your baby during birth.

False vs. early labor

A factor in the equation is also early labor vs. false labor. While some doctors are still not adhering to the recommendation made in a combined declaration by groups for medicine like the American Clinical Practice Guidelines and the Nation for Perinatal Prenatal Care, it is inappropriate to characterize active work till its cervix seems to be dilated by at least six centimeters at this point, this is to prevent increased dangers posed to the mother and the unborn child.

It is shown herein that following these recommendations is a secure and efficient strategy to lower the main, or first-time, cesarean delivery rate. This is false labor since You have a cervix not developing, and you are not in labor if you are not experiencing contractions that change your cervix in approximately an hour. Early labor is when your cervix dilates; however, you are still not six cm dilated. It's ideal for giving birth early, handled at home, where you can relax.

5.4 Upon leaving the Hospital

You will get guidelines about what to look for and when to go back after leaving the hospital. It is crucial to understand that numerous parents enter the facility only to be sent home in order to wait before returning to give birth. This could even be a little awkward and tiring emotionally. This is one of the examples that main causes why so numerous families decide to wait until after admission before telling their loved ones they are going to the hospital.

You can also be prescribed medicine to promote sleep or reduce your symptoms. You can also get advice on using over the pledge drugs to aid sleep. Be careful to seek counsel if you have not been given instructions on how to treat your symptoms.

5.5 Methods to Help Reduce the Number of False Alarms

Nobody wants you to be discharged from the medical center before or before labor has even begun. You may take certain steps to make sure, but once you traveled to that same hospital or location when you were born, you remain there until the delivery of your child.

Take a Childbirth Class

Childbirth classes are educational programs designed to help expectant parents prepare for the labor, delivery, and early postpartum care of their newborn. The classes may cover various topics, such as breathing and relaxation techniques, pain management options, breastfeeding basics, and newborn care. The benefits of attending childbirth classes include increased knowledge and confidence in coping with labor and delivery, improved communication and decision-making skills with healthcare providers, and opportunities to connect with other expectant parents.

By attending these classes, expectant parents can learn skills and strategies to manage childbirth's physical and emotional challenges, which can help reduce anxiety and improve overall birth outcomes. Additionally, attending childbirth classes can also help to prepare new parents for the transition to parenthood, offering practical advice and support in a safe and nurturing environment.

Hire a Doula

A doula has been specially trained to assist you and your young family in the months before delivery, through early labor and active labor, and in the first few weeks after delivery. This includes assisting you in identifying true vs. false labor. This can even include having a doula visit your home to help you time some contractions. They can also guide you on when you want to contact your doctor or return to the hospital.

Time Contractions

Contractions have a complexity that involves a great deal more than just time. Although timing contractions can seem simple, there is a secret to that which is superior learned in person. While a contraction timing tool is useful, it cannot substitute a medical professional who can assess the strength of your contractions.

Signs That May Indicate Labor

As a general rule, the signs of labor can vary from woman to woman and from pregnancy to pregnancy. Some women experience early signs of labor for several days or even weeks before labor actually begins, while others may experience no signs at all until labor is well underway. However, some common signs that may indicate the onset of labor include:

- Contractions: These are often described as a tightening or cramping sensation in the lower abdomen or back, which may become increasingly frequent and intense as labor progresses.
- Bloody show: This refers to the passage of a small amount of blood-tinged mucus from the cervix, which can be a sign that the cervix is beginning to dilate and efface in preparation for delivery.

- Water breaking: This refers to the rupture of the amniotic sac, which can result in a gush or trickle of fluid from the vagina.
- Lower back pain: Some women may experience pain or pressure in the lower back as a sign of labor.
- Nesting: Some women may experience a sudden burst of energy or the urge to organize and prepare for the baby's arrival.

It is important to note that these signs are not definitive and may not necessarily indicate the onset of labor. If your wife is experiencing any of these signs, it is important to contact her healthcare provider to determine whether she is in labor and to receive further guidance.

5.6 When to go Back to the Hospital

You will eventually need to go back to your birthplace. The easiest way to know when it's time is because when your signs of labor have progressed to the worsened, your contractions are more frequent, stronger, and further apart, or you meet any other requirements your physician has established. It would help if you kept an eye out for symptoms like:

- Vaginal bleeding;

- Contractions that are stronger, deeper, and closer together;

Return to that same hospital or birth site when your wife notices these symptoms. This might happen shortly after you've left the hospital, or it could happen weeks or days later. In all honesty, nobody can predict with certainty when it will occur. If you want to avoid coming to the hotel and waiting in triage until it is determined whether or not your wife is in labor, you can also request to come in for a brief check outside office hours with her physician. If a practitioner is open and has employees, many of them provide this service.

When you return to the hospital, you will again be subjected to the triage procedure. Your wife will be put in labor and permitted to deliver the baby if it is found that she is in labor. Do not forget that labor to procedure and each experiences the phases of labor at slightly different times and in different ways. Even within the same individual, it may change from pregnancy to pregnancy. Work together again and try not to stress out; each person on your squad wishes the ideal for your wife, you and your child.

5.7 How to Take Your Wife Completely by Surprise with A Babymoon

Have you ever heard of or been exposed to the babymoon idea? As its name implies, this trend is a means by which commemorates you and your partner will experience parenthood for the first time. It is gaining more and more popularity as time goes by. Even though the honeymoon is ended, there is another significant "moon" you can look forward to arranging your household expands. It doesn't matter if you're a first-time parent or have been a parent for a while. If you are expecting a child, we have some good news for you: there is another milestone "moon" that you can look forward to organizing.

Babymoon is a brief journey or vacation taken by a couple immediately preceding their child's birth. Before the birth of their kid, new parents, as well as those who have previously been parents, might consider taking their spouses on a "babymoon," which is short for "babymoon vacation." That brief window of time before your family grows is a wonderful opportunity to reconnect with yourself and your partner to strengthen your bond as a team responsible for raising children.

Babymoon is an excellent opportunity for expectant parents to enjoy some quality time spent collectively as a pair before the arrival of their first child, an event that will undoubtedly alter the dynamic of their relationship in several ways. You and your partner can celebrate the fact that you are expecting a child in many different ways. Many people have the misconception that a babymoon needs to incorporate a luxurious location comparable to going on a honeymoon, while in reality, there are a great number of distinct ways that you can rejoice in this beautiful period of your life.

Find something helpful for her when the delivery of the baby draws near.

It's wonderful when you can locate a present that reflects the two of you and your connection, but that doesn't mean that more practical presents aren't still welcome and appreciated. Purchasing your partner's maternity clothes can be an excellent method to demonstrate that you are planning and want them to continue to feel fashionable throughout their pregnancy.

Finding jeans or denim with a pregnancy waistband may serve as a terrific alternative, especially if your partner enjoys wearing slim or regular jeans. Expectant moms can look great in jeans just like everyone else, and the greatest maternity jeans are so well-designed that they can't even be distinguished from regular jeans at first glance!

When your partner is pregnant, it doesn't matter if she's in her first, second, or third trimester; the greatest pregnancy pants will make her seem hot from every perspective.

It is difficult to make a mistake with a tried-and-true piece of clothing like maternity jeans because they offer a fashion that is both comfy and functional. Maternity clothes come in a wide range of washes, from dark to light, and offer a long-lasting and stylish solution for women who want to show off their growing bellies without calling undue attention to themselves.

Choose a present that brings the two of you closer together as a pair.

Many consider a babymoon the last celebration a couple gets to have together before starting a family. Therefore, picking a sentimental item that speaks to you as a pair and is not connected to your soon-to-be-born baby girl or guy is only appropriate.

The acquisition of such a present may be accomplished in

various ways; nevertheless, if you want to go above and beyond, shopping online for initial necklaces is one of the best methods. It is possible to create a lovely memento of your life together by having a necklace crafted with either your initials or the initials of both you and your spouse. This will give them the means to carry you with them no matter where they go. In particular, your household expands, and having something to be a constant reminder of the unique spouse who helps them in every possible way and an initial necklace is a good example of this wonderful way to recognize the connection the two of you share.

Enchanting is a classic and sophisticated way to express affection for your spouse as you begin a new section inside your own life together. Whether they prefer to wear their initial necklace every day or only on special occasions, a jeweler is wonderful in demonstrating affection for your relationship.

Dote on her a little bit; nine months is a very long time

Even if there is a predetermined length of time for the babymoon, this does not imply that there are no other ways in which you and your partner can go the additional mile for your unborn child while carrying you. It is important to remember that pregnancy comes with its share of highs and lows; hence, it has more surprises and is never a bad thing in store to make the ride one or two additional pleasant.

One approach to show her you care is to treat her to a manicure regularly to enable her to look forward to showing off her stylish nail paint and feeling pampered. Take your wife to their favorite manicurist and ask if they offer gel manicures. Gel manicures protect the nails from damage and, with a top coat, can last significantly longer than regular polish. A gel manicure topped with an additional coat is an excellent way to compliment her new preferred pregnancy jeans and look wonderful with her daily clothes.

However, finding a way to pamper her during pregnancy is essential, so get creative if she'd rather not pay a visit to a nail technician. In the end, regardless of whether or if your partner enjoys getting a manicure or pedicure is a relaxing experience. A matter of taste; nonetheless, finding ways to treat her like a queen while she's carrying your child is essential.

When you are expecting a child, it may be a really exciting moment, but it's crucial to remember to still celebrate your relationship with your partner. Taking a babymoon together may serve as a wonderful way to celebrate your love while also being excited about what comes after this one stage of your life. You can do many things to bring it extra memorable. You can do many different things to honor this new chapter in your life, such as going on an amazing trip or buying unique presents that are a tribute to you and your significant other.

5.8 Is There Sexual Activity After Having a Baby?

According to a popular proverb, you will depart as a family when you go into the delivery room as a couple. It's also true that your connection with your partner won't be the same as it was before the pregnancy. After the birth of their child, many couples find that they cannot continue having sexual relations with one another. What are you supposed to do, being a guy like you?

It could take anywhere from four to six weeks for them to heal entirely, and even after that, it's possible that they won't be ready for sex yet. This depends on how they gave birth, whether vaginally or via cesarean section. The changing of hormones during breastfeeding may influence your partner's libido. By "affected," we mean that they will have less interest in engaging in sexual activity.

It is possible that they are not the only person who is not in the mood, which may come as a surprise to you. The late-night feedings and diaper changes may have left the two of you completely exhausted. It is entirely conceivable to be too exhausted for sexual activity. A period of drought could be easier to bear if one keeps in mind the following:

- The better news is that you might feel less irritated if you bear in mind that troubles with sex are usual for recuperating after giving birth, which is good news since it may help you feel less frustrated. Most women also experience some sex-related issues during this specific period. You could experience less anger and frustration if you keep this in mind.
- However, the majority of first-time moms continue their

sexual intercourse three months after they give birth. This is an encouraging statistic.

- A significant number of women report that they delay having sexual intercourse because they are afraid of becoming pregnant once again after having an abortion. It's possible that having a conversation with your partner about the different types of birth control might help them get in the groove.

- Your partner is going through substantial emotional and physical changes, which may affect their ability to have sex and willingness to do so. This may also affect your ability to have sex with them. These alterations could also affect their desire to have sexual encounters. Pay attention to how they feel about engaging in sexual activity again, and let them control the terms of your contact with them. Pay attention to how they feel about engaging in sexual activity again.

5.9 Some Travel Advice
Be intentional and familiar with your goals.

A babymoon does not need to be a luxurious experience. It may be as easy as leaving the children with the spouse's parents for the weekend or reserving a suite at one of the city's more upscale hotels. The most important thing is to turn off all electronic devices and consciously take pleasure in the time spent together as a pair.

Bear in mind that a "babymoon" does not always imply that only the parents-to-be will be doing any traveling, regardless of whether it is a "staycation" for the weekend or a "final chance to check off a favorite destination before the baby comes. According to experts, one couples journey to Morocco served as the family's "babymoon" after the birth of their third kid. That way, you would know that before you went back to traveling in a more relaxed manner for a bit with the new baby, you could make sure that you crossed off one of the places on your travel bucket list with the older kids. When you clearly understand the trip's objectives, you will be better able to devise a strategy that will result in a satisfied mother back at home.

Because of this, experts advise going with a travel advisor who is aware of the goals you have set for yourself and can help you achieve them. Someone knowledgeable in the wellness industry is the best person to work with if you want your babymoon to be focused on relaxing at a spa. Suppose you are searching for a vacation suitable for families yet allowing adults to have some time to themselves. In that case, you should consult an expert familiar with organizing luxurious family vacations.

Get ready to improve your flying skills.

Consider the discomforts associated with pregnancy since this is another piece of advice for those who travel while pregnant. Prolonged motion, such as a flight or a drive, might bring on or exacerbate various pregnancy-related symptoms. Imagine having pain in your back, swollen feet, and nausea. Always bring some water and food with you when you travel, and if you're going to fly, choose a seat on the aisle for easier access to the lavatory and carry some compression socks to prevent swollen ankles.

Safety Comes First

All expectant couples need to be fully educated and prepared to take any safety steps that may be required. While there are no parameters for how far you should travel or how long you should stay, experts want all expectant parents to be well-informed and ready to take any safety measures that may be necessary. Before departing on your babymoon, you

should research the health and safety standards, vaccination requirements, and cleaning procedures of each location you visit.

Be careful to only book your own time.

Even if your goal is to cross a location or activity off your bucket list, a travel expert warns against overscheduling your trip and packing more than needed in the available time. A babymoon is a time to put your feet up, read the book you've been meaning to get to, eat and pamper yourself.

5.10 Baby's Here: Now What?

The moment your baby is born and the hours that follow may be incredibly meaningful to you, but there is typically a lot going on during these times. What takes place in the moments immediately following the delivery of your child will be determined by how your child was born, as well as the health of both your child and your partner.

During the pregnancy, you and your pregnant spouse might find it helpful to discuss how the first few hours of the new baby's life might best be spent. For instance, you might consider the following topics:

- Ensure that your newborn has direct skin-to-skin contact with you

- Give your spouse time to rest and recover after the baby's delivery. Assist your partner in initiating breastfeeding if at all feasible.

- Assist your partner in feeding the baby with a bottle if you cannot nurse the child.

It is also important to discuss how and when you will get in touch with your family and friends, as well as when you will be able to receive guests.

After birth, direct skin-to-skin contact is encouraged.

In the first hour after birth, it is beneficial for your child to have skin-to-skin contact with you. It can assist with the following:

- keeping your baby warm

- keeping your infant from getting sick.

- maintaining stability in your baby's heart rate and breathing rate

- ensuring that your infant's blood sugar remains at a healthy level

- bonding.

It is beneficial for newborns to have direct skin-to-skin contact with their parents immediately after birth. When your partner has skin-to-skin contact with your baby, you might either place your hand on your baby or let your infant grab one of your fingers. In addition, if, for whatever reason, your partner is unable to have skin-to-skin contact with your baby, it will still be beneficial for your child to have skin-to-skin contact with you.

Even if your newborn requires more care or has to go to the neonatal intensive care unit (NICU) or a special care nursery after birth, you will still be able to have skin-to-skin contact with your child. Holding your baby's hand or placing your hands on your baby's head, feet, or back are all great ways to initiate skin-to-skin contact, especially if your baby is ill or was born prematurely. Inquire with the members of the NICU team about the possibility of having skin-to-skin contact with your infant. In the weeks after your baby is born, while they grow and develop, having skin-to-skin contact with you may aid with calming and sleeping, as well as brain development, soothing, and connecting.

Assisting the mother while she is breastfeeding

Breastfeeding is an activity that can be done in a group setting. Your encouragement and support throughout breastfeeding can make it easier for your spouse to initiate nursing and continue it for longer.

You can be of assistance by educating yourself on how to breastfeed by reading and viewing videos about the nursing process. You can also lend a hand by doing tasks such as changing your child's diaper and holding, cradling, or otherwise calming your child after being breastfed.

You can also provide your spouse with tangible assistance, such as a drink of water, an additional pillow, or anything else your partner may require. If your partner has difficulty nursing, you should reassure them that seeking further assistance in this endeavor is acceptable. You have several different avenues to get support:

- The hospital's midwives

- A lactation consultant in the medical center

- Your general practitioner or the child and family health nurse in your area

Assisting your partner in their recovery after giving birth

After the birth, you, your spouse, and your child will need time to heal from the physical and emotional impacts of the experience.

However, after the delivery of the baby, your partner, in particular, will require some time to relax and recuperate. This is because your partner will probably experience the following:

- feeling very weary

- have some bleeding from the vagina and discomfort in the area of the vaginal or cesarean wound

- suffer from after-paints and discomfort in the nipple or breast.

Getting hands-on with your newborn is one of the most effective methods to ensure your partner has a restful and speedy recovery after giving birth, regardless of whether the baby was delivered vaginally or via cesarean section. This may entail bathing your kid, changing their diapers, and bringing your child to your spouse so they can breastfeed them.

Concerning the care of a new infant, you could experience excitement, enthusiasm, or perhaps some anxiety. You can consult a midwife if unsure about actions to take in a given situation. Furthermore, if you or your partner have any questions about anything that occurred during the labor and delivery of the baby, it is a good idea to consult a midwife or doctor about it.

The recovery period following a cesarean section might last up to six weeks. In the first six weeks after delivery, if your partner requires a cesarean section, you may need to continue providing most of the newborn care while also tending to your partner's needs. It is possible that your plans for coming back to work will need to be altered or that you will need to make arrangements for your spouse to receive additional assistance.

Maintain regular check-ins with one another to determine what your spouse requires and desires, and work cooperatively to ensure your child's well-being throughout this time.

What to Expect After the Birth of the Baby for New Fathers

You are well aware that becoming a parent will change your life forever. You won't be able to find out how and in what ways it happened. Nothing can truly prepare you for the satisfactions and trials of becoming a parent. But being aware of what to anticipate at this point can help cut down on the number of significant shocks that lie ahead.

Before the baby is born, here is a sneak peek at how you and your partner's relationship, as well as your self-image, your ability to sleep, and your sexual life, may all be affected by the arrival of your new child.

And With That, We Are Now Three

Before the arrival of your child, you and your partner had more time to attend to the requirements of each other and to enjoy each other's company. Having a child allows you to reevaluate your top priorities and reduces your freedom and control over your life. After becoming a parent, it is easy to become preoccupied with one's new responsibilities as a mother or father. Keep in mind that you both started as a couple.

Instead of considering your child's birth to be the most important thing in your life, try to see it as something that will strengthen your relationship with your partner. As you ease into your new role as a parent, keep these things in mind:

- Emphasize the connection you share with your partner. Many professionals recommend that you and your partner devote some of your time to spending time together—just the two of you—about once every week or so. Sometimes this may consist of chatting over a cup of coffee or accompanying each other to the supermarket.

- Do not record who's turn to change the baby's diapers or do duties around the house. Instead, offer your assistance whenever it is required.

- Come to an understanding with your partner over allocating "me time." Most new mothers, particularly those with other children at home, may benefit from setting aside time each week to walk, read a book, or sit quietly.

Conclusion

As we come to the end of this book, we hope that you have found it to be a useful guide for your journey as an expectant father. The experiences of pregnancy and childbirth can be overwhelming, but with proper preparation and support, you can play an active and positive role in this process.

Throughout this book, we have covered many important topics, including how to support your partner during pregnancy, prepare for childbirth, and navigate the postpartum period. We have also highlighted the many positive aspects of fatherhood, such as the opportunity to bond with your child and the chance to form a deeper connection with your partner.

We hope this book has given you the tools and information you need to feel confident and prepared as you embark on this new journey. Remember, being an expectant father is a wonderful experience, filled with love, joy, and the chance to create a lifelong bond with your child. With patience, empathy, and a willingness to learn, you can be a supportive and involved partner to your wife and a loving and attentive father to your child.

Thank you for reading, and we wish you all the best as you begin this exciting new chapter of your life!

Printed in Great Britain
by Amazon

22858235R00077